AAT

ASSESSMENT KIT

Intermediate Unit 7

Reports and Returns

May 2002 edition

- Practice activities
- Two practice devolved assessments
- One trial run devolved assessment
- The AAT's sample simulation for this Unit
- New guidance on the preparation of portfolios

FOR 2002 AND 2003 SKILLS BASED ASSESSMENTS

BPP Publishing
May 2002

First edition May 1998
Fifth edition May 2002

ISBN 0 7517 6426 4 (Previous edition 0 7517 6406 X)

British Library Cataloguing-in-Publication Data
A catalogue record for this book
is available from the British Library

Published by

BPP Publishing Limited
Aldine House, Aldine Place
London W12 8AW

www.bpp.com

Printed in Great Britain by WM Print
45 - 47 Frederick Street
Walsall, West Midlands WS2 9NE

We are grateful to the Lead Body for Accounting for permission to reproduce extracts from the Standards of Competence for Accounting.

CONTENTS

Page

Activities   Answers

Practice activities are short activities directly related to the actual content of the BPP Interactive Text. They are graded pre-assessment and assessment.

Practice devolved assessments consist of a number of tasks covering certain areas of the Standards of Competence but are not full assessments.

Trial run devolved assessments are of similar scope to full simulations.

Lecturers' resource pack activities are practice activities and assessments for lecturers to set in class or for homework. The answers are given in the BPP Lecturers' Resource Pack.

ORDER FORM

REVIEW FORM & FREE PRIZE DRAW

Activity Checklist/Index

HOW TO USE THIS ASSESSMENT KIT

Aims of this Assessment Kit

> To provide the knowledge and practice to help you succeed in the assessment for Intermediate Unit 7 *Reports and Returns*.

To succeed in the assessment you need a thorough understanding in all areas covered by the standards of competence.

> To tie in with the other components of the BPP Effective Study Package to ensure you have the best possible chance of success.

Interactive Text
This covers all you need to know for assessment for Unit 7. Icons clearly mark key areas of the text. Numerous activities throughout the text help you practise what you have just learnt.

Assessment Kit
When you have understood and practised the material in the Interactive Text, you will have the knowledge and experience to tackle this Assessment Kit for Unit 7. This aims to get you through the assessment, whether in the form of a simulation or workplace assessment. It contains the AAT's Sample Simulation for Unit 7 plus other simulations.

Passcards
These short memorable notes are focused on key topics for Unit 7, designed to remind you of what the Interactive Text has taught you.

Recommended approach to this Assessment Kit

(a) To achieve competence in all units you need to be able to do **everything** specified by the standards. Study the Interactive Text very carefully and do not skip any of it.

(b) Learning is an **active** process. Do **all** the activities as you work through the Interactive Text so you can be sure you really understand what you have read.

(c) After you have covered the material in the Interactive Text, work through this **Assessment Kit**.

(d) Try the **Practice Activities**. These are linked into each chapter of the Interactive Text, and are designed to reinforce your learning and consolidate the practice that you have had doing the activities in the Interactive Text. Depending on their difficulty, they are graded as Pre-assessment or Assessment.

(e) Then attempt the **Practice Devolved Assessments**. These are designed to test your competence in certain key areas of the Standards of Competence and will give you practice at completing a number of tasks based upon the same data.

(f) Next do the **Trial Run Devolved Assessment**. This is designed to cover the areas you might see when you do a full devolved assessment.

(g) Finally try the AAT's **Sample Simulation** which gives you the clearest idea of what a full assessment will be like.

Remember this is a **practical** course.

(a)   Try to relate the material to your experience in the workplace or any other work experience you may have had.

(b)   Try to make as many links as you can to your study of the other units at this level.

Lecturers' Resource Pack activities

At the back of this Kit we have included a number of chapter-linked activities without answers. We have also included a trial run devolved assessment without answers. The answers for this section are in the BPP Lecturers' Resource Pack for this Unit.

Stop press

The AAT is planning to change the terminology used for assessments in the following ways:

(a)   Central assessments to be called exam based testing
(b)   Devolved assessments to be called skills based testing

As the plans had not been finalised at the time of going to press, the 2002 editions of BPP titles will continue to refer to central and devolved assessments.

UNIT 7 STANDARDS OF COMPETENCE

The structure of the Standards for Unit 7

The Unit commences with a statement of the **knowledge and understanding** which underpin competence in the unit's elements.

The unit is then divided into **elements of competence** describing activities which the individual should be able to perform.

Each element includes:

(a) A set of **performance criteria** which define what constitutes competent performance

(b) A **range statement** which defines the situations, contexts, methods etc in which competence should be displayed

(c) **Evidence requirements**, which state that competence must be demonstrated consistently, over an appropriate time scale with evidence of performance being provided from the appropriate sources

(d) **Sources of evidence**, being suggestions of ways in which you can find evidence to demonstrate that competence

The elements of competence for Unit 7 *Preparing Reports and Returns* are set out below. Knowledge and understanding required for the Unit as a whole are listed first, followed by the performance criteria, range statements, evidence requirements and sources of evidence for each element. Performance criteria are cross-referenced to chapters in the Unit 7 *Reports and Returns* Interactive Text.

Unit 7 Preparing reports and returns

What is the unit about?

This unit relates to the preparation of reports and returns from information obtained from all relevant sources. You are required to calculate ratios and performance indicators and present the information according to the appropriate conventions and definitions to either management or outside agencies, including the VAT office. The unit is also concerned with your communication responsibilities which include obtaining authorisation before despatching reports, seeking guidance from the VAT office and presenting reports and returns in the appropriate manner.

The business environment

- Main sources of relevant government statistics (Elements 7.1 & 7.2)

- Awareness of relevant performance and quality measures (Element 7.1)

- Main types of outside organisations requiring reports and returns: regulatory; grant awarding; information collecting; trade associations (Element 7.2)

- Basic law and practice relating to all issues covered in the range statement and referred to in the performance criteria. Specific issues include: the classification of types of supply; registration requirements; the form of VAT invoices; tax points (Element 7.3)

- Sources of information on VAT: Customs and Excise Guide (Element 7.3)

- Administration of VAT: enforcement (Element 7.3)

- Special schemes: annual accounting; cash accounting; bad debt relief (Element 7.3)

Accounting techniques

- Use of standard units of inputs and outputs (Element 7.1 & 7.3)

- Time series analysis (Element 7.1)

- Use of index numbers (Element 7.1)

- Main types of performance indicators: productivity; cost per unit; resource utilisation; profitability (Elements 7.1 & 7.2)

- Ratios: gross profit margin; net profit margin; return on capital employed (Elements 7.1 & 7.2)

- Tabulation of accounting and other quantitative information (Elements 7.1 & 7.2)

- Methods of presenting information: written reports; diagrammatic; tabular (Elements 7.1 & 7.2)

The organisation

- Understanding of the ways the accounting systems of an organisation are affected by its organisational structure, its administrative systems and procedures and the nature of its business transactions (Elements 7.1, 7.2 & 7.3)

- Understanding of the purpose and structure of reporting systems within the organisation (Element 7.1)

- Background understanding that a variety of outside agencies may require reports and returns from organisations and that these requirements must be built into administrative and accounting systems and procedures (Element 7.2 & 7.3)

- Background understanding that recording and accounting practices may vary between organisations and different parts of organisations (Elements 7.1, 7.2 & 7.3)

- An understanding of the basis of the relationship between the organisation and the VAT office (Element 7.3)

Element 7.1   Prepare and present periodic performance reports

Performance criteria	Chapters in the Interactive Text
1 Information derived from different units of the organisation is consolidated into the appropriate form	9
2 Information derived from different information systems within the organisation is correctly reconciled	9
3 When comparing results over time an appropriate method, which allows for changing price levels, is used	7
4 Transactions between separate units of the organisation are accounted for in accordance with the organisation's procedures	10
5 Ratios and performance indicators are accurately calculated in accordance with the organisation's procedures	9, 11
6 Reports are prepared in the appropriate form and presented to management within required timescales	2 – 6, 8

Range statement

1   Information: costs; revenue

2   Ratios: gross profit margin; net profit margin; return on capital employed

3   Performance indicators: productivity; cost per unit; resource utilisation; profitability

4   Methods of presenting information: written report containing diagrams; table

Evidence requirements

- Competence must be demonstrated consistently, over an appropriate timescale with evidence of performance being provided of periodic performance reports.

Sources of evidence

(these are examples of sources of evidence, but you may be able to identify other, appropriate sources)

- **Observed performance**, eg Consolidating information in the appropriate form; reconciling information from different information systems; comparing results over time; calculating ratios and performance indicators; preparing reports; oral presentation of periodic performance reports.

- **Work produced by the candidate**, eg periodic performance reports containing written information, charts and graphs; calculations of ratios and performance indicators; correspondence between different units of the organisation.

- **Authenticated testimonies from relevant witnesses.**

- **Personal accounts of competence, eg report of performance.**

- **Other sources of evidence to prove competence or knowledge and understanding where it is not apparent from performance**, eg performance in independent assessment; performance in simulation; responses to verbal questioning.

Element 7.2   Prepare reports and returns for outside agencies

Performance criteria	Chapters in the Interactive Text
1 Relevant information is identified, collated and presented in accordance with the conventions and definitions used by outside agencies	2, 8
2 Calculations of ratios and performance indicators are accurate	9
3 Authorisation for the despatch of completed reports and returns is sought from the appropriate person	1
4 Reports and returns are presented in accordance with outside agencies' requirements and deadlines	2, 8

Range statement

1   Ratios: gross profit margin; net profit margin; return on capital employed

2   Reports and returns: written report; return on standard form

Evidence requirements

- Competence must be demonstrated consistently, over an appropriate timescale with evidence of performance being provided of reports and returns being presented to outside agencies.

Sources of evidence

(these are examples of sources of evidence, but you may be able to identify other, appropriate sources)

- **Observed performance**, eg collating information; presenting information; preparing information; preparing reports and returns; calculating ratios and performance indicators; seeking authorisation for the despatch of reports and returns.

- **Work produced by the candidate**, eg written reports; standard returns; authorisation for despatch; calculations of ratios and performance indicators; correspondence with outside agencies.

- **Authenticated testimonies from relevant witnesses.**

- **Personal accounts of competence**, eg report of performance.

- **Other sources of evidence to prove competence or knowledge and understanding where it is not apparent from performance**, eg reports and working papers; performance in independent assessment; performance in simulation; responses to questions.

Element 7.3 Prepare VAT returns

Performance criteria	Chapters in the Interactive Text
1 VAT returns are correctly completed using data from the appropriate recording systems and are submitted within the statutory time limits	12
2 Relevant inputs and outputs are correctly identified and calculated	12, 13
3 Submissions are made in accordance with current legislation	13
4 Guidance is sought from the VAT office when required, in a professional manner	13

Range statement

1 Recording systems: computerised ledgers; manual control account; cash book

2 Inputs and outputs: standard supplies; exempt supplies; zero rated supplies; imports; exports

Evidence requirements

- Competence must be demonstrated consistently, with evidence of performance being provided of VAT returns with backup documentary evidence.

Sources of evidence

(these are examples of sources of evidence, but you may be able to identify other, appropriate sources)

- **Observed performance**, eg completing VAT returns; calculating inputs and outputs; seeking guidance from the VAT office.

- **Work produced by the candidate**, eg completed VAT returns; calculating inputs and outputs; seeking guidance from the VAT office.

- **Authenticated testimonies from relevant witnesses.**

- **Personal accounts of competence**, eg report of performance.

- **Other sources of evidence to prove competence or knowledge and understanding where it is not apparent from performance**, eg performance in simulation; performance in independent assessment; responses to questions.

ASSESSMENT STRATEGY

This Unit is assessed by **devolved assessment/skills based testing only**.

Devolved assessment

Devolved assessment is a means of collecting evidence of your ability to **carry out practical activities** and to **operate effectively in the conditions of the workplace** to the standards required. Evidence may be collected at your place of work, or at an Approved Assessment Centre by means of simulations of workplace activity, or by a combination of these methods.

If the Approved Assessment Centre is a **workplace**, you may be observed carrying out accounting activities as part of your normal work routine. You should collect documentary evidence of the work you have done, or contributed to, in an **accounting portfolio**. Evidence collected in a portfolio can be assessed in addition to observed performance or where it is not possible to assess by observation.

Where the Approved Assessment Centre is a **college or training organisation**, devolved assessment will be by means of a combination of the following.

(a) Documentary evidence of activities carried out at the workplace, collected by you in an **accounting portfolio**.

(b) Realistic **simulations** of workplace activities. These simulations may take the form of case studies and in-tray exercises and involve the use of primary documents and reference sources.

(c) **Projects and assignments** designed to assess the Standards of Competence.

If you are unable to provide workplace evidence you will be able to complete the assessment requirements by the alternative methods listed above.

Possible assessment methods

Where possible, evidence should be collected in the workplace, but this may not be a practical prospect for you. Equally, where workplace evidence can be gathered it may not cover all elements. The AAT regards performance evidence from simulations, case studies, projects and assignments as an acceptable substitute for performance at work, provided that they are based on the Standards and, as far as possible, on workplace practice.

There are a number of methods of assessing accounting competence. The list below is not exhaustive, nor is it prescriptive. Some methods have limited applicability, but others are capable of being expanded to provide challenging tests of competence.

Assessment method	Suitable for assessing
Performance of an accounting task either in the workplace or by simulation: eg preparing and processing documents, posting entries, making adjustments, balancing, calculating, analysing information etc by manual or computerised processes	**Basic task competence.** Adding supplementary oral questioning may help to draw out underpinning knowledge and understanding and highlight your ability to deal with contingencies and unexpected occurrences
General case studies. These are broader than simulations. They include more background information about the system and business environment	Ability to **analyse a system** and suggest ways of modifying it. It could take the form of a written report, with or without the addition of oral or written questions
Accounting problems/cases: eg a list of balances that require adjustments and the preparation of final accounts	Understanding of the **general principles of accounting** as applied to a particular case or topic
Preparation of flowcharts/diagrams. To illustrate an actual (or simulated) accounting procedure	**Understanding of the logic** behind a procedure, of controls, and of relationships between departments and procedures. Questions on the flow chart or diagram can provide evidence of underpinning knowledge and understanding
Interpretation of accounting information from an actual or simulated situation. The assessment could include non-financial information and written or oral questioning	**Interpretative competence**
Preparation of written reports on an actual or simulated situation	**Written communication skills**
Analysis of critical incidents, problems encountered, achievements	Your ability to handle **contingencies**
Listing of likely errors eg preparing a list of the main types of errors likely to occur in an actual or simulated procedure	Appreciation of the range of **contingencies** likely to be encountered. Oral or written questioning would be a useful supplement to the list
Outlining the organisation's policies, guidelines and regulations	Performance criteria relating to these aspects of competence. It also provides evidence of competence in **researching information**
Objective tests and short-answer questions	**Specific knowledge**
In-tray exercises	Your **task-management ability** as well as technical competence
Supervisors' reports	**General job competence**, personal effectiveness, reliability, accuracy, and time management. Reports need to be related specifically to the Standards of Competence

Assessment method	Suitable for assessing
Analysis of work logbooks/diaries	**Personal effectiveness**, time management etc. It may usefully be supplemented with oral questioning
Formal written answers to questions	Knowledge and understanding of the **general accounting environment** and its impact on particular units of competence
Oral questioning	**Knowledge and understanding** across the range of competence including organisational procedures, methods of dealing with unusual cases, contingencies and so on. It is often used in conjunction with other methods

Simulations

Simulations will generally be based round a single scenario containing information relevant to all three elements of the Unit. You will need to select the items of information relevant to each task. **Simulations for the new Unit 7 will be approximately 3^1/$_2$ hours long.**

BUILDING YOUR PORTFOLIO

What is a portfolio?

A portfolio is a collection of work that demonstrates what the owner can do. In AAT language the portfolio demonstrates **competence**.

A painter will have a collection of his paintings to exhibit in a gallery, an advertising executive will have a range of advertisements and ideas that she has produced to show to a prospective client. Both the collection of paintings and the advertisements form the portfolio of that artist or advertising executive.

Your portfolio will be unique to you just as the portfolio of the artist will be unique because no one will paint the same range of pictures in the same way. It is a very personal collection of your work and should be treated as a **confidential** record.

What evidence should a portfolio include?

No two portfolios will be the same but by following some simple guidelines you can decide which of the following suggestions will be appropriate in your case.

(a) **Your current CV**

This should be at the front. It will give your personal details as well as brief descriptions of posts you have held with the most recent one shown first.

(b) **References and testimonials**

References from previous employers may be included especially those of which you are particularly proud.

(c) **Your current job description**

You should emphasise financial **responsibilities and duties**.

(d) **Your student record sheets**

These should be supplied by AAT when you begin your studies, and your training provider should also have some if necessary.

(e) **Evidence from your current workplace**

This could take many forms including **letters, memos, reports** you have written, **copies of accounts** or **reconciliations** you have prepared, **discrepancies** you have investigated etc. Remember to obtain permission to include the evidence from your line manager because some records may be sensitive. Discuss the performance criteria that are listed in your Student Record Sheets with your training provider and employer, and think of other evidence that could be appropriate to you.

(f) **Evidence from your social activities**

For example you may be the treasurer of a club in which case examples of your cash and banking records could be appropriate.

(g) **Evidence from your studies**

Few students are able to satisfy all the requirements of competence by workplace evidence alone. They therefore rely on simulations to provide the remaining evidence to complete a unit. If you are not working or not working in a relevant post, then you may need to rely more heavily on simulations as a source of evidence.

(h) **Additional work**

Your training provider may give you work that specifically targets one or a group of performance criteria in order to complete a unit. It could take the form of questions, presentations or demonstrations. Each training provider will approach this in a different way.

(i) **Evidence from a previous workplace**

This evidence may be difficult to obtain and should be used with caution because it must satisfy the 'rules' of evidence, that is it must be current. Only rely on this as evidence if you have changed jobs recently.

(j) **Prior achievements**

For example you may have already completed the health and safety unit during a previous course of study, and therefore there is no need to repeat this work. Advise your training provider who will check to ensure that it is the same unit and record it as complete if appropriate.

How should it be presented?

As you assemble the evidence remember to **make a note** of it on your Student Record Sheet in the space provided and **cross reference** it. In this way it is easy to check to see if your evidence is **appropriate**. Remember one piece of evidence may satisfy a number of performance criteria so remember to check this thoroughly and discuss it with your training provider if in doubt.

To keep all your evidence together a ring binder or lever arch file is a good means of storage.

When should evidence be assembled?

You should begin to assemble evidence **as soon as you have registered as a student**. **Don't leave it all** until the last few weeks of your studies, because you may miss vital deadlines and your resulting certificate sent by the AAT may not include all the units you have completed. Give yourself and your training provider time to examine your portfolio and report your results to AAT at regular intervals. In this way the task of assembling the portfolio will be spread out over a longer period of time and will be presented in a more professional manner.

What are the key criteria that the portfolio must fulfil?

As you assemble your evidence bear in mind that it must be:

- **Valid.** It must relate to the Standards.

- **Authentic.** It must be your own work.

- **Current.** It must refer to your current or most recent job.

- **Sufficient.** It must meet all the performance criteria by the time you have completed your portfolio.

What are the most important elements in a portfolio that covers Unit 7?

You should remember that the unit is about the **preparation** of **reports** and **returns**. Therefore you need to produce evidence not only demonstrating that you can carry out certain tasks, but also you must be able to show that you can prepare the relevant reports and returns.

For Element 7.1 *Prepare and present periodic performance reports* you not only need to show that you can produce periodic performance reports containing written information, you also need to demonstrate that you have used this information in order to produce charts and graphs. You will also need to provide evidence of having calculated ratios and performance indicators.

To fulfil the requirements of Element 7.2 *Prepare reports and returns for outside agencies* you need to demonstrate that you have completed standard returns and written reports for external bodies. You also need to provide evidence of correspondence with these bodies and evidence that you have sought authorisation for the despatch of any such correspondence.

For Element 7.3 *Prepare VAT returns* you need to show evidence of completed VAT returns (showing how you have calculated any input and output VAT). You will also need to show evidence of having sought guidance from the VAT office where necessary.

Finally

Remember that the portfolio is **your property** and **your responsibility**. Not only could it be presented to the external verifier before your award can be confirmed; it could be used when you are seeking **promotion** or applying for a more senior and better paid post elsewhere. How your portfolio is presented can say as much about you as the evidence inside.

Practice activities

1 *The organisation, accounting and reporting*

1   DISTINGUISH   **Pre-assessment**

List four ways in which it is possible to distinguish organisations from each other.

2   PAYROLL   **Pre-assessment**

You work in the payroll department of Ketchgate Hospital. At the end of each month you prepare payroll summaries which are submitted to cost centre managers. What must you do **each month before** you submit the payroll summaries to the relevant cost centre managers?

3   REPORTS   **Pre-assessment**

List four types of business report that are produced by an organisation's accounting information system.

2   *Business and accounting information*

4   DATA AND INFORMATION   **Pre-assessment**

Distinguish between data and information.

5   INTERNAL SOURCES   **Pre-assessment**

Give four examples of internal sources of business information.

6   COST ACCOUNTING   **Pre-assessment**

Cost and management accounting is concerned entirely with providing information in the form of periodic performance reports or special 'one-off reports. Give six examples of cost and management accounting information.

3 *Statistical information*

7 STATEMENTS **Pre-assessment**

Comment on each of the following statements.

(a) Aircraft passenger deaths were up by 10% over last year, so air travel is getting more dangerous.

(b) The fact that the pass rate in the exam decreased from 44% to 41% shows that a higher standard was expected at this sitting.

(c) Shopper to supermarket manager: 'It says in the newspapers that inflation is coming down, so your prices ought to be falling if they reflect national trends, as you claim'.

8 DATA **Pre-assessment**

Distinguish between primary data and secondary data.

9 SECONDARY DATA **Pre-assessment**

What is the main advantage of secondary data?

BPP PUBLISHING

4 *Presenting information: graphs*

10 INDEPENDENT VARIABLE   Pre-assessment

What is an independent variable and which axis on a graph represents it?

11 SCATTERGRAPH   Pre-assessment

What is a scattergraph?

12 BLANKS   Pre-assessment

The **upper quartile** is the value of the item which is .... % of the way through the cumulative frequencies. It is also known as the .... quartile.

The **lower quartile** is the value of the item which is .... % of the way through the cumulative frequencies. It is also known as the .... quartile.

5 *Presenting information: tables and charts*

13 SIGNIFICANT DIGITS   **Pre-assessment**

State 2,197.283 correct to:

(a) Six significant digits
(b) Five significant digits
(c) Four significant digits

14 DECIMAL PLACES   **Pre-assessment**

State 38.17832 correct to:

(a) Three decimal places
(b) Two decimal places
(c) One decimal place

BPP PUBLISHING

6 *Averages and time series*

15 FORMULA **Pre-assessment**

What is the mathematical formula used to calculate the arithmetic mean of a frequency distribution? (Explain the symbols that are used in the formula you have stated.)

16 AVERAGES **Assessment**

Write brief notes explaining the following terms to a colleague.

(a) The mean
(b) The median
(c) Time series

7   *Using index numbers*

17   PRICE INDEX   Pre-assessment

What is a price index?

18   SALES INDEX   Assessment

Sales for V plc over the last five years were as follows.

Year	Sales (£'000)
20X5	35
20X6	42
20X7	40
20X8	45
20X9	50

V plc's managing director decides that he wants to set up a **sales index** (ie an index which measures how sales have done from year to year), using 20X5 as the base year. The £35,000 of sales in 20X5 is given the index 100%. What are the indices for the other years?

19   MACHINE PRICES   Assessment

An index of machine prices has year 1 as the base year, with an index number of 100. By the end of year 9 the index had risen to 180 and by the end of year 14 it had risen by another 18 points.

What was the percentage increase in machine prices between years 9 and 14?

8 Writing reports and completing forms

20 FORMS   **Assessment**

Which one item of information which should have been entered on the form below by the employer has not been? (All items of information and figures which are included on the form can be assumed to be correct.)

Inland Revenue   *Details of employee leaving work*   **P45**
Copy for Tax Office   **Part 1**

		District number	Reference number
1	PAYE Reference	135	C 2721

2 Employee's National Insurance number   RC 28 72 94 D

                                           (Mr Mrs Miss Ms)

3 Surname (in capitals)   FREDERICK   MR

   First name(s) (in capitals)   JOHN

		Day	Month	Year
4	Leaving date (in figures)	31	5	20 X8

5 Tax Code at leaving date. *If week 1 or Month 1 basis applies, write 'X' in the box marked Week 1 or Month 1*

  Code: 370   Week 1 or Month 1

6 Last entries on *Deductions Working Sheet* (P11) **Complete only if Tax Code is cumulative.** *Make no entry here if Week 1 or Month 1 basis applies. Go to item 7.*

                                        Week   Month

    Week or month number   2

    Total pay to date   £ 3,000 00 p

    Total tax to date   £ 579 83 p

7 This employment pay and tax. ■ *No entry needed if Tax Code is cumulative and amounts are same as item 6 entry.*

    Total pay in this employment   £   p

    Total tax in this employment   £   p

8	Works number/Payroll number	414	9	Department or branch if any	

10 Employee's private address and Postcode

    17 REEDS ROAD
    SEDGEWORTH
    RN7 4TR

11 I certify that the details entered above in items 1 to 9 are correct

    Employer's name, address and Postcode

    WARBLERS (SEDGEWORTH) LTD
    EXE ROAD, SEDGEWORTH
    RN12 1BN

    Date   31/5/X8

To the employer   For Tax Office use

- Complete this form following the 'Employee leaving' instructions in the *Employer's quick Guide to PAYE and NICs* (cards CWG1). Make sure the details are clear on all four parts of this form. Make sure your name and address is shown on Parts 1 and 1A.
- Detach Part 1 and send it to your Tax Office immediately.
- Hand Parts 1A, 2 and 3 (unseparated) to your employee when he or she leaves
- If the employee has died, write 'D' in this box and send all three parts of this form (unseparated) to your Tax Office immediately.

P45   BMSD 3/97

9 Reporting performance

21 COST CENTRE   Pre-assessment

Explain what you understand by the term **cost centre** and give four examples of cost centres.

22 TRANSFER PRICE   Pre-assessment

(a) What is a **transfer price**?

(b) What basis might be used to set a transfer price?

23 CONSOLIDATION OF INFORMATION   Assessment

Consolidated departmental trading and profit and loss accounts for Special Ltd are as follows:

SPECIAL LIMITED
DEPARTMENTAL TRADING AND PROFIT AND LOSS ACCOUNTS
FOR THE YEAR ENDED 31 AUGUST 20X0

	Dept A		Dept B	
	£	£	£	£
Sales		720,000		1,080,000 [(1)]
Cost of sales:				
Opening stock	144,000		180,000	
Purchases	420,000 [(2)]		648,000	
	564,000		828,000	
Less closing stock	156,000		216,000	
		408,000		612,000
Gross profit		312,000		468,000
Less expenses:				
Selling & distribution	91,200		136,800	
Administration	69,800		105,800	
Lighting & heating	4,000		19,200	
Rent & rates	76,000		38,000	
		241,000		299,800
Net profit		71,000		168,200

Note

(1) Includes sales to Dept A at cost of £92,000.

(2) This figure includes purchases from Dept B of £92,000.

Task

Calculate the consolidated trading and profit and loss account for Special Limited for the year ended 31 August 20X0 showing clearly any adjustments which should be made.

10 Measuring performance

| 24 | **PRODUCTION AND PRODUCTIVITY** | **Pre-assessment** |

Distinguish between the terms **production** and **productivity**.

| 25 | **ROCE** | **Pre-assessment** |

What do you understand by the term **return on capital employed**?

| 26 | **NET PROFIT MARGIN** | **Assessment** |

S plc compares its 20X2 results with 20X1 results as follows.

	20X2	*20X1*
	£	£
Sales	800,000	600,000
Cost of sales		
Direct materials	200,000	100,000
Direct labour	200,000	150,000
Production overhead	110,000	100,000
Marketing overhead	210,000	175,000
	720,000	525,000
Profit	80,000	75,000

Calculate the net profit margins for S plc for 20X1 and 20X2.

11 The VAT charge and VAT records

27 JULIE **Assessment**

In January 2003, Julie makes a table using wood from a tree which fell down in her garden during a winter storm. In February 2003, she sells it to John's Frantic Furniture Ltd for £200.

The company buys materials to varnish and polish the table from Thomas for £70.50 including VAT. The company sells the table to M&F plc for £600 excluding VAT in March 2003. Jo buys the table from M&F plc for £1,000 inclusive of VAT in April 2003.

All of the above persons except Julie and Jo are registered for VAT and account for VAT quarterly and have tax periods running to the end of June, September, December and March.

Task

Show all payments to HM Customs & Excise arising from these transactions, the relevant VAT return and the due dates.

28 COCO LTD **Assessment**

CoCo Ltd has made sales and purchases as indicated by the following documents.

CoCo LTD			
Job Ltd		CoCo House	
2 High Street		Gosforth	
Newcastle		G4 0BB	
NE7 2LH		VAT reg no GB 212 7924 36	
Invoice no. 501			
Date: 3 January 2003			
Tax point: 3 January 2003			
		VAT rate	
		%	£
Sale of 300 cups		17.5	300.00
Sale of 400 saucers		17.5	450.00
Total excluding VAT			750.00
Total VAT at 17.5%			131.25
Total payable within 30 days			881.25

CoCo LTD

The Dublin Company
29 Grafton Street
Dublin
Ireland

CoCo House
Gosforth
G4 0BB
VAT reg no GB 212 7924 36

VAT reg no IR 99369326 5
Invoice no. 502
Date: 4 January 2003
Tax point: 4 January 2003

	VAT rate %	£
Sale of 500 cups	0.0	500.00
Sale of 2,000 plates	0.0	4,000.00
Total excluding VAT		4,500.00
Total VAT at 0.0%		0.00
Total payable within 30 days		4,500.00

CoCo LTD

Supplies plc
2 Main Street
Oldham
OL4 7TC

CoCo House
Gosforth
G4 0BB
VAT reg no GB 212 7924 36

Invoice no. 503
Date: 1 February 2003
Tax point: 1 February 2003

	VAT rate %	£
Sale of 700 saucers	17.5	1,050.00
Sale of 3,000 cups	17.5	3,000.00
Total excluding VAT		4,050.00
Total VAT at 17.5%		708.75
Total payable within 30 days		4,758.75

CoCo LTD

Job Ltd
2 High Street
Newcastle
NE7 2LH
Credit note no. 2
Date: 10 February 2003

CoCo House
Gosforth
G4 0BB
VAT reg no GB 212 7924 36

	VAT rate %	£
Return of defective goods: 30 cups		
(invoice no. 501, date 3.1.03)	17.5	30.00
Total credited excluding VAT		30.00
Total VAT credited at 17.5%		5.25
Total credited including VAT		35.25

CLAY SUPPLIES PLC

10 Speldhurst Road, Chiswick W4 00X
VAT registration number 187 2392 49

Invoice to: CoCo Ltd
CoCo House
Gosforth
G4 0BB

Date: 21 February 2003
Tax point: 21 February 2003
Invoice no. 996

	£
4 tonnes of clay	4,000.00
VAT at 17.5%	700.00
Amount payable	4,700.00

Terms: strictly net 30 days

INVOICE
GLAZE SUPPLIES LTD

To: CoCo Ltd
27 New Road   CoCo House
Manchester   Gosforth
M14 4XX   G4 0BB

VAT reg no 162 4327 56
Date: 28 February 2003
Tax point: 28 February 2003
Invoice no. 0002

	VAT rate %	Net £	VAT £	Gross £
100L Class A glaze	17.5	2,700.00	472.50	3,172.50
5L Class B glaze	17.5	80.00	14.00	94.00
		2,780.00	486.50	3,266.50

£3,266.50 is payable by 7 March 2003. Interest will be charged thereafter at 1.5% per month.

Input VAT for the VAT period ended 31 December 2002 was overstated by £600.

Task

Complete the following VAT return for CoCo Ltd.

Value Added Tax Return
For the period
01 01 03 to 31 03 03

For Official Use

Registration number
212 7924 36

Period
03 03

You could be liable to a financial penalty if your completed return and all the VAT payable are not received by the due date.

Due date: 30 04 03

For Official Use

ATTENTION

If this return and any tax due are not received by the due date you may be liable to a surcharge.

If you make supplies of goods to another EC Member State you are required to complete an EC Sales List (VAT 101).

CoCo Ltd
Coco House
GOSFORTH
G4 0BB

Your VAT Office telephone number is 0123-4567

Before you fill in this form please read the notes on the back and the VAT Leaflet *"Filling in your VAT return"*.
Fill in all boxes clearly in ink, and write 'none' where necessary. Don't put a dash or leave any box blank. If there are no pence write "00" in the pence column. Do not enter more than one amount in any box.

For official use			£	p
	VAT due in this period on sales and other outputs	1	834	75
	VAT due in this period on acquisitions from other EC Member States	2	NONE	
	Total VAT due (the sum of boxes 1 and 2)	3	834	75
	VAT reclaimed in this period on purchases and other inputs (including acquisitions from the EC)	4	586	50
	Net VAT to be paid to Customs or reclaimed by you (Difference between boxes 3 and 4)	5	248	25
	Total value of sales and all other outputs excluding any VAT. Include your box 8 figure	6	9270	00
	Total value of purchases and all other inputs excluding any VAT. Include your box 9 figure	7	6780	00
	Total value of all supplies of goods and related services, excluding any VAT, to other EC Member States	8	4,500	00
	Total value of all acquisitions of goods and related services, excluding any VAT, from other EC Member States	9	NONE	00

If you are enclosing a payment please tick this box.

DECLARATION: You, or someone on your behalf, must sign below.

I, ... declare that the
(Full name of signatory in BLOCK LETTERS)
information given above is true and complete.

Signature.. Date .... 19 ....
A false declaration can result in prosecution.

29   CLIPPER LTD   **Assessment**

Clipper Ltd holds the following invoices from suppliers.

(a)

VAT reg no 446 9989 57			Jupiter plc
Date: 4 January 2003			1 London Road
Tax point: 4 January 2003			Reading
Invoice no.			RL3 7CM

Clippers Ltd
13 Gale Road
Chester-le-Street
NE1 1LB

Sales of goods

Type	Quantity	VAT rate %	Net £
Earrings	2,700	17.5	1,350.00
Earring studs	2,800	17.5	1,400.00
			2,750.00
VAT at 17.5%			457.19
Payable within 60 days			3,207.19
Less 5% discount if paid within 14 days			137.50
			3,069.69

(b)

HILLSIDE LTD

'The Glasgow Based Suppler of Quality Jewellery Items'

VAT reg no 337 4849 26

Clipper Ltd
13 Gale Road
Chester-le-Street
NE1 1LB

Invoice no. 0010
Date: 10 August 2002
Tax point: 10 August 2002

	£
Sale of 4,000 Jewellery boxes	8,000
VAT at 17.5%	1,450
Total	9,450

Terms: strictly net 30 days

BPP PUBLISHING

(c)

GENEROUS PLC

11 Low Fell
Leeds
LS1 XY2

Clipper Ltd
13 Gale Road
Chester-le-Street
NE1 1LB

Invoice no: 2221
Date: 12 December 2002
Tax point: 12 December 2002

	Net £	*VAT* £	*Total* £
4,000 Earrings	2,000.00	350.00	2,350.00
8,000 Brooches	2,500.00	437.50	2,937.50
3,500 'How to make Jewellery' books	5,000.00	0.00	5,000.00
	9,500.00	787.50	10,287.50

(d)

JEWELS & CO
101 High Street, Gateshead NE2 22P

VAT reg no 499 3493 27

Date: 2 January 2003

30 necklaces sold for £95.00 including VAT at 17.5%.

For each of the above invoices, state whether it is a valid VAT invoice. Give your reasons.

12 The computation and administration of VAT

30   ZAG PLC   **Assessment**

Zag plc had the following sales and purchases in the three months ended 30 June 2003. All amounts exclude any VAT, and all transactions were with United Kingdom traders.

	£	
Sales		
Standard rated	877,500	*153,562. 50*
Zero rated	462,150	
Exempt	327,600	
Purchases		
Standard rated		
Attributable to taxable supplies	585,000	*102,375*
Attributable to exempt supplies	146,250	
Unattributable	468,000	
Zero rated	8,190	
Exempt	15,405	

Task

Compute the figures which would be entered in boxes 1 to 5 of Zag plc's VAT return for the period (copy enclosed).

Value Added Tax Return
For the period
30 03 03 to 30 06 03

Registration number	Period
483 8611 98	06 03

You could be liable to a financial penalty if your completed return and all the VAT payable are not received by the due date.

Due date: 31 07 03

For Official Use

ZAG PLC
32 CASE STREET
ZEDTOWN
ZY4 3JN

If you have a general enquiry or need advice please call our National Advice Service on 0845 010 9000

ATTENTION

If this return and any tax due are not received by the due date you may be liable to a surcharge.

If you make supplies of goods to another EC Member State you are required to complete an EC Sales List (VAT 101).

Before you fill in this form please read the notes on the back and the VAT Leaflet *"Filling in your VAT return"*. Fill in all boxes clearly in ink, and write 'none' where necessary. Don't put a dash or leave any box blank. If there are no pence write "00" in the pence column. Do not enter more than one amount in any box.

For official use	Description	Box	£	p
	VAT due in this period on sales and other outputs	1	153,562	50
	VAT due in this period on acquisitions from other EC Member States	2	NONE	
	Total VAT due (the sum of boxes 1 and 2)	3	153,562	50
	VAT reclaimed in this period on purchases and other inputs (including acquisitions from the EC)	4	168,714	00
	Net VAT to be paid to Customs or reclaimed by you (Difference between boxes 3 and 4)	5	15,151	50
	Total value of sales and all other outputs excluding any VAT. Include your box 8 figure	6	1,667,250	00
	Total value of purchases and all other inputs excluding any VAT. Include your box 9 figure	7	1,222,845	00
	Total value of all supplies of goods and related services, excluding any VAT, to other EC Member States	8	NONE	00
	Total value of all acquisitions of goods and related services, excluding any VAT, from other EC Member States	9	NONE	00

If you are enclosing a payment please tick this box.

DECLARATION: You, or someone on your behalf, must sign below.

I, ... (Full name of signatory in BLOCK LETTERS) declare that the information given above is true and complete.

Signature .... Date 19

A false declaration can result in prosecution.

31   PAUL LUCAS   Assessment

Paul Lucas is a trader who uses the cash accounting scheme. Some of his sales are standard rated, some are zero rated and some are exempt. Transactions for which the sale, the purchase or the receipt or payment of cash fell in the three months ended 31 March 2003 are as follows. All amounts include any VAT. No input VAT is attributable to any particular type of supply. There are no transactions with anyone outside the United Kingdom.

Date of transaction	Date cash received or paid	VAT rate %	Amount £		
Sales					
20.12.02	1.1.03	17.5	310.50	46.24	264.26
21.12.02	2.1.03	17.5	410.75	61.18	349.57
2.1.03	5.1.03	17.5	719.25	107.12	612.13
3.1.03	4.1.03	0.0	640.30		
10.1.03	20.1.03	0.0	721.50		
15.1.03	1.2.03	17.5	400.00	59.57	340.43
20.1.03	1.2.03	Exempt	190.50		
29.1.03	7.2.03	0.0	207.50		
2.2.03	7.2.03	17.5	300.00	44.68	255.32
4.2.03	12.2.03	Exempt	400.00		
14.2.03	1.3.03	Exempt	525.50		
21.2.03	2.3.03	0.0	275.50		
1.3.03	12.4.03	Exempt	802.35 ✗		
15.3.03	31.3.03	17.5	299.99	44.68	255.31
30.3.03	4.4.03	17.5	700.00 ✗		
Purchases					
27.12.02	10.1.03	17.5	400.00	59.57	340.43
2.1.03	4.1.03	17.5	527.13	78.51	448.62
23.1.03	5.2.03	0.0	702.10		
7.2.03	20.2.03	17.5	600.00	89.36	510.64
12.2.03	1.3.03	Exempt	212.21		
13.3.03	2.4.03	17.5	800.00 ✗		
30.3.03	3.4.03	17.5	199.00 ✗		

Paul also took fuel from the business (without payment) for use in his 2.500 cc petrol engined car, which he does not drive for business purposes. The scale charge is £422. 62.85

Task

Complete the following VAT return for Paul Lucas.

Value Added Tax Return

For the period
01 01 03 to 31 03 03

For Official Use

Registration number
483 8611 98

Period
03 03

You could be liable to a financial penalty if your completed return and all the VAT payable are not received by the due date.

Due date: 30 04 03

For Official Use

MR PAUL LUCAS
12 HALDANE ROAD
BRADFORD
BR4 3JN

Your VAT Office telephone number is 0123-4567

ATTENTION

If this return and any tax due are not received by the due date you may be liable to a surcharge.

If you make supplies of goods to another EC Member State you are required to complete an EC Sales List (VAT 101).

Before you fill in this form please read the notes on the back and the VAT Leaflet *"Filling in your VAT return"*.
Fill in all boxes clearly in ink, and write 'none' where necessary. Don't put a dash or leave any box blank. If there are no pence write "00" in the pence column. Do not enter more than one amount in any box.

For official use			£	p
	VAT due in this period on sales and other outputs	**1**	426	32
	VAT due in this period on acquisitions from other EC Member States	**2**	NONE	
	Total VAT due (the sum of boxes 1 and 2)	**3**	426	32
	VAT reclaimed in this period on purchases and other inputs (including acquisitions from the EC)	**4**	227	44
	Net VAT to be paid to Customs or reclaimed by you (Difference between boxes 3 and 4)	**5**	198	88
	Total value of sales and all other outputs excluding any VAT. Include your box 8 figure	**6**	5396	00
	Total value of purchases and all other inputs excluding any VAT. Include your box 9 figure	**7**	2214	00
	Total value of all supplies of goods and related services, excluding any VAT, to other EC Member States	**8**	NONE	00
	Total value of all acquisitions of goods and related services, excluding any VAT, from other EC Member States	**9**	NONE	00

If you are enclosing a payment please tick this box.	DECLARATION: You, or someone on your behalf, must sign below.
	I, ... declare that the
	(Full name of signatory in BLOCK LETTERS)
	information given above is true and complete.
	Signature.. Date .... 19 ....
	A false declaration can result in prosecution.

32 MAYFAIR PLC   Assessment

In one VAT period, Mayfair plc has the following transactions in goods which would be sold at the standard rate if supplied in the UK. All amounts listed below exclude any VAT, and all goods sold are sent to the buyers' countries by Mayfair plc.

(a) Sells goods to a French customer for £1,500. The customer is not registered for VAT, and the relevant French VAT rate is 25%

(b) Buys goods from a UK supplier for £19,250

(c) Buys goods from a VAT registered Italian supplier for £6,000. The invoice shows Mayfair plc's VAT registration number and the goods are sent direct to Mayfair's premises in London by the supplier

(d) Sells goods to an American customer for £5,275

(e) Sells goods to a German customer for £14,200. The customer's VAT registration number is shown on the sales invoice

Task

Compute the VAT payable to or recoverable from HM Customs & Excise for the period.

General – preparing reports and returns

The following data is required for Practice activities 33-35.

Comma Limited		Income Statement		
	September 20X2		Year to date	
	Budget £	Actual £	Budget £	Actual £
Gross sales	2,207,000	2,079,480	23,519,000	24,498,743
Discounts	(64,000)	(60,510)	(684,000)	(703,871)
Net sales	2,143,000	2,018,970	22,835,000	23,794,872
Standard cost	1,123,500	1,022,777	11,567,000	12,314,815
Variances	171,000	241,240	1,888,000	2,271,729
Other costs	187,400	227,004	2,734,000	1,911,008
Inter-company contribution	(119,400)	(178,273)	(1,600,400)	(1,296,234)
Total cost of sales	1,362,500	1,312,748	14,588,600	15,201,318
Manufacturing margin	780,500	706,222	8,246,400	8,593,554
Direct sales	70,000	57,271	682,000	672,827
Promotion	61,000	45,843	632,000	637,221
Other marketing	76,600	73,490	1,172,000	1,247,160
General admin	181,000	181,221	1,997,400	1,886,662
Data processing	68,000	70,147	721,000	713,072
Loan interest	62,000	65,014	710,000	702,942
	518,600	492,986	5,914,400	5,859,884
Inter-company contribution	(40,000)	(20,102)	(490,000)	(189,722)
Total overheads	478,600	472,884	5,424,400	5,670,162
Operating income	301,900	233,338	2,822,000	2,923,392
Inter-company (net)	(19,000)	21,270	(210,000)	(22,972)
Income before taxes	282,900	254,608	2,612,000	2,900,420
Taxes on income	(151,000)	(103,700)	(1,397,000)	(1,411,670)
Net income	131,900	150,908	1,215,000	1,488,750

NET SALES BY GEOGRAPHICAL MARKET

	20X1	20W6
United Kingdom	12,248,721	9,272,845
Canada	1,722,400	1,888,245
Eire	2,014,522	-
Germany	3,604,745	1,457,208
France	2,308,722	1,200,405
Nigeria	1,521,223	1,721,542
Other EC	2,418,717	894,281
USA	3,401,972	2,841,470
Other non-EC	1,182,718	1,141,722
	30,423,740	20,417,718

Note. Eire, Germany and France were all members of the European Union in both 20W6 and 20X1, as was the United Kingdom.

TOTAL NET SALES

	£
20W6	20,417,718
20W7	22,084,165
20W8	23,782,722
20W9	25,621,481
20X0	28,088,390
20X1	30,423,740
20X2 Sept YTD	23,794,872

Average number of employees

	Full-time	Part-time
20W6	694	38
20W7	721	37
20W8	742	44
20W9	765	48
20X0	870	53
20X1	852	57
20X2 Sept YTD	842	61

33 INCOME STATEMENT   Assessment

Prepare a simplified income statement for Comma Ltd showing the budgeted and actual results for the month of September 20X2, and the nine months to September 20X2, with both £million (rounded as considered appropriate but with no amount shown to more than three digits) and percentage columns (net sales = 100%; round to the nearest one per cent). The income statement should include the following lines.

Net sales
Less: Standard cost
           Variances
           Other costs
           Inter-company contribution
Manufacturing margin
Selling expenses
Administrative expenses
Inter-company contribution
Operating income
Inter-company (net)
Income before tax
Tax
Net income

For the purposes of comparison, your statement should also incorporate the following previous year actual figures, rounded as appropriate and additionally showing the manufacturing margin and operating income expressed as a percentage of net sales.

September 20X1

	£
Net sales	1,850,972
Manufacturing margin	611,227
Operating income	209,944

9 months to September 20X2

	£
Net sales	22,402,106
Manufacturing margin	7,827,435
Operating income	2,210,810

34   PIE CHART   Assessment

Prepare a pie chart comparing the split of Comma Ltd's net sales between its major geographical markets in 20W6 and 20X1. The major geographical markets should be classified as follows.

UK
Exports: European Union
           North America
           Other

35   BAR CHART   Assessment

Prepare a bar chart for Comma Ltd showing net sales per full-time employee (in 20X2 pounds) over the period 20W6 to 20X1. A part-time employee is to be treated as equivalent to one half of a full time employee for this purpose. The average Retail Prices Index figures below are to be used for the purpose of adjusting the relevant figures to 20X2 pounds.

Year	RPI average
20W6	128.2
20W7	132.7
20W8	139.5
20W9	146.2
20X0	150.7
20X1	157.8
20X2	164.9

The following data relate to Practice activities 36-42.

EMERALD TAXIS LTD
MANAGEMENT ACCOUNTS
CUMULATIVE REPORT FOR THE SIX MONTHS ENDED 30 JUNE 20X7

Vehicle	1	2	3	4	5	6	7	8	Total
Registration number	J761 SET	K937 SET	H976 WSF	J172 PED	H127 PDM	G789 JDM	J129 HBD	H969 MDD	-
Local authority reference	SC84	SC101	SC105	SC126	SC191	SC213	SC220	SC225	-
Operating mileage	16,100	17,900	15,200	17,500	12,100	14,900	16,912	17,500	128,112
Operating hours	1,638	1,710	1,490	1,650	1,360	1,575	1,620	1,640	12,683
Operating days	181	180	175	181	160	175	180	181	1,413
Income (£)	14,500	16,289	13,376	16,100	10,285	13,410	15,400	15,900	115,260
Expenditure									
	£	£	£	£	£	£	£	£	£
Road fund licence	75	75	75	75	75	75	75	75	600
Local authority registration	65	65	65	65	65	65	65	65	520
Insurance	610	700	590	620	575	550	610	560	4,815
Maintenance: fixed	60	64	60	77	95	70	85	80	591
variable	60	65	70	68	300	70	75	72	780
Wages	6,500	6,800	5,960	6,600	5,440	6,300	6,480	6,560	50,640
Tyres	80	85	75	85	65	81	87	90	648
Fuel	1,210	1,561	1,220	1,310	875	1,077	1,185	1,310	9,748
Depreciation	1,250	1,050	900	1,000	875	800	1,050	850	7,775
Administration	2,180	2,180	2,180	2,180	2,180	2,180	2,180	2,180	17,440
	12,090	12,645	11,195	12,080	10,545	11,268	11,892	11,842	93,557
Profit/(loss)	2,410	3,644	2,181	4,020	(260)	2,142	3,508	4,058	21,703

Variable costs comprise: fuel, wages, tyres plus variable maintenance costs.

Fixed costs comprise: road fund licence, Local Authority Registration fee, insurance, depreciation, administration plus fixed maintenance costs.

Contribution = income – variable costs.

MONTHLY ANALYSIS OF INCOME AND EXPENDITURE

	Income	*Expenditure*
	£	£
January	18,894	15,310
February	18,405	15,425
March	18,820	14,875
April	18,774	17,322
May	19,942	14,285
June 20X7	20,425	16,340
	115,260	93,557

36 KEY FINANCIAL RATIOS   Assessment

Prepare the following key financial ratios for each vehicle and for the business overall for the six months ended 30 June 20X7. Calculate the ratios to the nearest penny, or in the case of percentages, to one decimal place.

(a) Income per operating mile
(b) Income per operating hour
(c) Income per operating day
(d) Contribution per operating mile
(e) Contribution per operating hour
(f) Contribution per operating day
(g) Variable costs per operating mile
(h) Variable costs per operating hour
(i) Variable costs per operating day
(j) Fixed costs per operating mile
(k) Fixed costs per operating hour
(l) Fixed costs per operating day
(m) Net profit (loss) per operating mile
(n) Net profit (loss) per operating hour
(o) Net profit (loss) per operating day
(p) Percentage net profit to income

37 GRAPH   Assessment

Prepare an appropriate graph or chart showing the analysis of total turnover for the period into variable costs, fixed costs and net profit. You are not required to show the results for individual vehicles on the graph or chart.

38 TABLE   Assessment

Prepare a table showing the performance ranking of the vehicles on the basis of net profit/(loss) per operating day.

39 STATEMENT   Assessment

The owner of Emerald Taxis is planning to add a further vehicle to his fleet of cars. He anticipates that the new vehicle will operate for 36,500 miles per annum.

Prepare a statement to estimate the annual income and costs for the new vehicle using, as a basis, the average of your figures for the key indicators you have prepared for the six months ended 30 June 20X7 (answer to Practice activity 36).

Assume that the fixed costs for the vehicle are the same as the average fixed costs for the current vehicles.

40   RPI   Assessment

Over the past five years the annual income of Emerald Taxis has been as follows.

	£
20X2	153,640
20X3	167,040
20X4	185,600
20X5	201,000
20X6	215,000

The RPI for the period 20X2-20X6 was as follows.

20X2	139.2
20X3	141.9
20X4	146.0
20X5	150.7
20X6	155.1

Convert the figures to real terms based on 20X6. Include the real annual year-on-year growth in turnover in your analysis.

41   REAL TERMS   Assessment

Using your answer to Practice activity 40, present the actual and real terms income figures for the period 20X2 to 20X6 in the form of a clearly labelled compound bar chart.

42   FORMS   Assessment

Complete the form below.

NATIONAL TAXI FEDERATION
RETURN FOR SIX MONTHS ENDED 30 JUNE 20X7

Company name: Emerald Taxis Limited
Membership number: EM002

Performance statistics:	*This period*	*20X6 full year*	*NTF 20X6 average*
Average revenue per vehicle operating day	....	£78.02	£79.70
Average total costs per vehicle operating day	....	£61.07	£60.14
Average revenue per operating mile	....	£0.88	£0.87
Average total costs per operating mile	....	£0.68	£0.67
Net profit as percentage of total revenue	....	17.1%	22.9%
Average mileage per operating day	....	88.66 miles	91.84 miles
Average mileage per operating hour	....	10.01 miles	9.75 miles

Signed: _____ Date: _____

Please submit this form to NTF Head Office as soon as possible.

General – Preparing VAT returns

The following data relate to Practice activities 43-51

As the accounts clerk at Tonk plc, you have been supplied with the following documents from which to prepare the company's VAT account. Also required is the VAT return for the three months ended 30 November 20X7. Assume that no further documents will be issued in connection with any of these transactions. You are warned that some invoices contain errors (which you need to detect).

TONK PLC
1 Plink Lane, Infertown. IN2 4DA
VAT reg no 154 9131 32

Invoice no. 572
Date: 4 September 20X7
Tax point: 4 September 20X7

To: Bar plc
        32 Stoke Street
        London NW12

	VAT rate	
	%	£
Sales of goods		
3,000 small suitcases	17.5	33,750.00
4,500 handbags	17.5	15,840.00
Total excluding VAT		49,590.00
Total VAT at 17.5%		8,504.68
Total payable within 30 days		58,094.68
Less 2% discount if paid within 10 days		991.80
Total payable within 10 days		57,102.88

TONK PLC
1 Plink Lane, Infertown. IN2 4DA
VAT reg no 154 9131 32

Invoice no. 573
Date: 12 September 20X7
Tax point: 12 September 20X7

To: Cormick Ltd
        63 Saddle Road
        Gulltown GL4 3CE

	VAT rate	
	%	£
Sales of goods		
2,000 trunks	17.5	38,000.00
7,000 shopping bags	17.5	14,000.00
Total excluding VAT		52,000.00
Total VAT at 17.5%	9,100	10,400.00
Total payable within 30 days, strictly net	61,100	62,400.00

TONK PLC
1 Plink Lane, Infertown. IN2 4DA
VAT reg no 154 9131 32

Invoice no. 574
Date: 3 October 20X7
Tax point: 3 October 20X7

To: Work plc
      99 Mark Lane
      Cartown CA1 9TP

	VAT rate	
	%	£
Sales of goods		
7,200 large suitcases	17.5	106,992.00
6,350 handbags	17.5	22,352.00
		129,344.00
Less 5% quantity discount		6,467.20
Total excluding VAT		122,876.80
Total VAT at 17.5%		18,431.52
Total payable within 30 days, strictly net		141,308.32

handwritten: 21,503.44 / 144,380.24

TONK PLC
1 Plink Lane, Infertown. IN2 4DA
VAT reg no 154 9131 32

Invoice no. 575
Date: 12 November 20X7
Tax point: 12 November 20X7

To: Monet plc
      39 Giro Street
      Bingotown BN6 2BC

	VAT rate	
	%	£
Sales of goods		
7,000 small suitcases	17.5	78,750.00
10,000 briefcases	17.5	158,700.00
Total excluding VAT		237,450.00
Total VAT at 17.5%		40,722.67
Total payable within 30 days		278,172.67
Less 2% discount if paid within 10 days		4,749.00
Total payable within 10 days		273,423.67

TONK PLC

1 Plink Lane, Infertown. IN2 4DA

VAT reg no 154 9131 32

Credit note no. 34

Date: 3 November 20X7

Tax point: 3 November 20X7

To: Sole plc
14 Power Street
Abbatown AB4 3BZ

Credit in respect of returned defective goods (invoice number 520; invoice date 1 July 20X7)

	VAT rate %	£
125 handbags	17.5	440.00
VAT at 17.5%		77.00
Total credit		517.00

TONK PLC

MEMORANDUM

To: Accounts clerk
From: Credit controller
Date: 2 October 20X7

Please write off the following two debts.

Debtor	Date payment due	Net £	VAT £	Gross £
Off Ltd	1.8.X7	2,000	350	2,350
Trib Ltd	14.1.X7	3,800	665	4,465

TONK PLC

MEMORANDUM

To: Accounts clerk
From: Finance director
Date: 4 November 20X7

Our auditors have found errors in our VAT accounting in a previous period. Output VAT was overstated by £2,500, and input VAT was overstated by £1,600. Please take the necessary corrective action.

VAT reg no 110 2511 35
Date: 12 October 20X7
Tax point: 12 October 20X7
Invoice no. 88577
To: Tonk plc
          1 Plink Lane
          Infertown IN2 4DA

TARSKI PLC
79 Reff Road
Selltown
SL2 9AT

	Net £	VAT rate %	VAT £
Sales of goods			
10,000 small suitcases	60,000.00	17.5	10,500.00
10,000 large suitcases	80,000.00	17.5	14,000.00
4,200 briefcases	30,660.00	17.5	5,365.50
Total excluding VAT	170,660.00		29,865.50
Total VAT at 17.5%	29,865.50		
Total payable within 30 days	200,525.50		

COURSE LTD
35 Work Street, Infertown IN3 7ET
VAT reg no 624 0668 24

15 October 20X7

Sale of 2,000 steel corner brackets: £83.60 including VAT at 17.5%.

SILK LTD
74 Hull Street, Infertown IN1 5DD
VAT reg no 281 8238 13

Date of supply

This is a less detailed invoice for VAT purposes.

Sale of 3,500 brass clips: £270.25 including VAT at 17.5%.

VAT reg no 110 2511 35
Date: 5 November 20X7
Credit note no. 324
To: Tonk plc
          1 Plink Lane
          Infertown IN2 4DA

TARSKI PLC
79 Reff Road
Selltown
SL2 9AT

CREDIT NOTE
(Invoice no. 88577, date 12 October 20X7)

	£
200 defective small suitcases returned	1,200.00
VAT at 17.5%	210.00
Gross credit	1,410.00

TONK PLC
EXPENSES CLAIM

Name: A Spender   Three months ended: 30.11.X7

	Net £	VAT £	Gross £
Business entertaining			
(VAT invoice attached)	300.00	52.50	352.50
Call from public telephone★	5.11	0.89	6.00
Car park fee★	15.32	2.68	18.00
Car park fee★	25.54	4.46	30.00
	345.97	60.53	406.50

★ No invoice or receipt issued
Authorised: A Manager

---

43 ERRORS   **Pre-assessment**

Outline the errors which you have detected in the documents supplied to you.

Practice activities 44-51 are to be completed assuming invoices corrected for the above errors have been reissued by Tonk plc.

44 OUTPUT VAT   **Pre-assessment**

Calculate Tonk plc's output VAT for the 3 months ended 30 November 20X7.

45 INPUT VAT   **Pre-assessment**

Calculate Tonk plc's input VAT for the 3 months ended 30 November 20X7.

46 NET TURNOVER   **Pre-assessment**

Calculate Tonk plc's total net turnover for the 3 months ended 30 November 20X7.

47 NET PURCHASES   **Pre-assessment**

Calculate Tonk plc's total net purchases for the 3 months ended 30 November 20X7.

48 NET ERROR   **Pre-assessment**

What is the net error relating to the previous VAT accounting period? How is it accounted for?

49 VAT ACCOUNT   **Pre-assessment**

Prepare the VAT account for the VAT period from September to November 20X7.

50 VAT RETURN   **Pre-assessment**

Prepare Tonk plc's VAT return for the 3 months ended 30 November 20X7 (using the results from Practice activity 49). A blank VAT return is provided below.

Value Added Tax Return

For the period

to

For Official Use

Registration number

Period

You could be liable to a financial penalty if your completed return and all the VAT payable are not received by the due date.

Due date:

For Official Use	

ADDRESS

If you have a general enquiry or need advice please call our National Advice Service on 0845 010 9000

ATTENTION

If this return and any tax due are not received by the due date you may be liable to a surcharge.

If you make supplies of goods to another EC Member State you are required to complete an EC Sales List (VAT 101).

Before you fill in this form please read the notes on the back and the VAT Leaflet *"Filling in your VAT return"*.
Fill in all boxes clearly in ink, and write 'none' where necessary. Don't put a dash or leave any box blank. If there are no pence write "00" in the pence column. Do not enter more than one amount in any box.

For official use			£	p
	VAT due in this period on sales and other outputs	1		
	VAT due in this period on acquisitions from other EC Member States	2		
	Total VAT due (the sum of boxes 1 and 2)	3		
	VAT reclaimed in this period on purchases and other inputs (including acquisitions from the EC)	4		
	Net VAT to be paid to Customs or reclaimed by you (Difference between boxes 3 and 4)	5		
	Total value of sales and all other outputs excluding any VAT. Include your box 8 figure	6		00
	Total value of purchases and all other inputs excluding any VAT. Include your box 9 figure	7		00
	Total value of all supplies of goods and related services, excluding any VAT, to other EC Member States	8		00
	Total value of all acquisitions of goods and related services, excluding any VAT, from other EC Member States	9		00

If you are enclosing a payment please tick this box.	DECLARATION: You, or someone on your behalf, must sign below.
	I, _____ declare that the
	(Full name of signatory in BLOCK LETTERS)
	information given above is true and complete.
	Signature _____ Date _____ 19
	A false declaration can result in prosecution.

51 DATE

Pre-assessment

State the date on which the VAT return is due to be received by Customs & Excise and on which date the overall VAT due will be paid to Customs.

Practice devolved assessments

37

Practice devolved assessment
1 Grady's Tutorial College

Performance criteria

The following performance criteria are covered in this Practice devolved assessment.

Element 7.1: Prepare and present periodic performance reports

1 Information derived from different units of the organisation is consolidated into the appropriate form.

2 Information derived from different information systems within the organisation is correctly reconciled.

3 When comparing results over time an appropriate method which allows for changing price levels is used.

4 Transactions between separate units of the organisation are accounted for in accordance with the organisation's procedures.

5 Ratios and performance indicators are accurately calculated in accordance with the organisation's procedures.

6 Reports are prepared in the appropriate form and presented to management within required timescales.

Element 7.2: Prepare reports and returns for outside agencies

1 Relevant information is identified, collated and presented in accordance with the conventions and definitions used by outside agencies.

2 Calculations of ratios and performance indicators are accurate.

3 Authorisation for the despatch of completed reports and returns is sought from the appropriate person.

4 Reports and returns are presented in accordance with outside agencies' requirements and deadlines.

Practice devolved assessment 1 Grady's Tutorial College

Instructions

This Assessment is designed to test your ability to prepare and present periodic performance reports and to prepare returns for outside agencies.

You are provided with data on the situation which you must use to complete the tasks listed. You are advised to read through the whole of the Assessment before commencing as all of the information may be of value and is not necessarily supplied in the sequence in which you might wish to deal with it. Part of your answer will require filling in a form on pages 45-49. You should complete the other tasks using your own paper.

You are allowed 2½ hours to complete your work.

A high level of accuracy is required. Check your work carefully. Correcting fluid may be used but should be used in moderation. Errors should be crossed out neatly and clearly. You should write in black ink, not pencil. Do not use any additional notes or books during this Practice devolved assessment. **A full answer to this Assessment is provided on page 125**. Do not turn to the suggested answer until you have completed all parts of the Assessment.

GRADY'S TUTORIAL COLLEGE

THE SITUATION

You are employed on a temporary assignment at Grady's Tutorial College. The College was set up in 20W8 and provides training courses, particularly for those wishing to return to work after a career break. Since 20X0, the college has also operated a small bookshop which sells mainly to course registrants but also to members of the public.

It is 12 April 20X4. Kim Harvey, the Financial Controller, hands to you some Office for National Statistics forms (see pages 44 to 49) which she received some time ago. At 5.30pm today, Kim, who needs to authorise the form, is leaving to go on a 10-day holiday. She asks if you would make sure that the forms are available for her to sign on her return from holiday.

Kim's telephone number at the college is 020-7711 4240 (Fax: 020-7711 4200).

The business has two divisions, called College Division (courses) and Bookshop (book sales). The accounting year end is 31 March.

The following table shows 'year-to-date' (YTD) figures for the business as at the end of each quarter in the year ending 31 March 20X4. These figures have been extracted from management accounts.

	30 June 20X3 *YTD* £	*30 Sept 20X3* *YTD* £	*31 Dec 20X3* *YTD* £	*31 March 20X4* *YTD* £
College Division				
Turnover	124,694	269,818	422,629	583,636
Direct costs	64,128	130,813	199,207	270,010
Other operating costs	22,031	43,498	72,882	97,509
Bookshop				
Turnover	12,721	28,223	46,931	71,094
Cost of sales	8,081	17,710	29,614	44,829
Staff costs	4,211	8,321	12,600	17,014
Other operating costs	2,412	4,401	6,589	9,420

Bookshop turnover includes books removed from the shop by members of College Division for their own use in course teaching. These books are invoiced at the full cover price to College Division, which has included them in 'other operating costs'. The average mark-up on the cost of books is 35%. The amounts of such interdivisional sales were as follows in the year to March 20X4.

Interdivisional book sales (at cover price): Year to March 20X4

Month	£	*Month*	£
Apr	205	Oct	234
May	110	Nov	121
Jun	20	Dec	333
Jul	312	Jan	394
Aug	333	Feb	481
Sep	214	Mar	192

Staff

College Division has employed 10 full-time members of staff (6 women and 4 men) and 1 part-time male member of staff throughout the whole of the year to 31 March 20X4. In

41

the same year, the bookshop has employed 1 full-time male staff member and 1 part-time female staff member, who started her job at the beginning of July 20X3.

Fixed assets

The following information has been extracted from the fixed asset register of Grady's Tutorial College.

	Land and buildings £	Plant and machinery £	Motor vehicles £	Office equipment £	Total £
Cost					
At 1 January 20X4	154,500	9,840	27,900	10,240	202,480
Additions	56,250	2,840	9,890	1,280	70,260
Disposals	-	(4,465)	(14,700)	(2,980)	(22,145)
At 31 March 20X4	210,750	8,215	23,090	8,540	250,595
Depreciation					
At 1 January 20X4	-	6,720	19,220	5,745	31,685
Charge for quarter	-	355	1,720	540	2,615
Disposals	-	(3,465)	(10,200)	(940)	(14,605)
At 31 March 20X4	-	3,610	10,740	5,345	19,695

Of the additions to land and buildings shown above, £32,150 was spent in buying a small building adjacent to the college. The remainder of these additions was in respect of improvements to the building in order to convert it to lecture room accommodation.

Certain fixed assets were sold, all for cash, in the quarter to 31 March 20X4. The debit entries in the cash book in respect of these sales are summarised below.

	£
Land and buildings	-
Plant and machinery	1,400
Motor vehicles	5,200
Office equipment	1,655

Tasks

1   Complete the Office for National Statistics forms in accordance with the accompanying notes (see pages 44 to 49).

2   State how much time is available for the ONS forms to be completed. State what action you would take to ensure that the forms are submitted on time.

3   Kim also requires you to set out in a table various items of information specified below for the following four periods.

   (a)   Quarter ending 30 June 20X3
   (b)   Quarter ending 30 September 20X3
   (c)   Quarter ending 31 December 20X3
   (d)   Quarter ending 31 March 20X4

   The information required is as follows. (Design your table with care before you begin this task.)

College Division

Turnover★
Direct costs★
Other operating costs★
Contribution★
Direct costs as % of turnover
Other operating costs as % of turnover
Contribution as % of turnover

★ in £'000 to one decimal place

Notes. Contribution = Turnover – (Direct costs + Other operating costs)

Bookshop

Turnover (including sales to College Division)
Cost of sales★
Staff costs★
Other operating costs★
Gross profit★
Contribution★
Gross profit percentage (ie as % of turnover)
Sales per staff member
Contribution as % of turnover

★ in £'000 to one decimal place

Notes. Gross profit = Turnover – Cost of sales
Contribution = Gross profit – (Staff costs + Other operating costs)

For the purpose of calculating numbers of staff members in this task, a part-time staff member is treated as equivalent to one half of a full-time member of staff.

4   Present the following ratios and percentages for each of the four quarters to 31 March 20X4, as calculated in Task (3) above, in an appropriate graphical format.

(a)   College Division:
Direct costs as % of turnover
Other operating costs as % of turnover
Contribution as % of turnover

(b)   Bookshop:
Gross profit percentage
Sales per staff member

5   An issue raised at a management meeting has been that of whether it is possible to measure the productivity of the teaching staff at Grady's Tutorial College. This has proved to be a contentious matter. You have been invited to attend the next management meeting to make a contribution to this discussion.

In preparation for the meeting, outline briefly different ways in which the productivity of the teaching staff might be measured, indicating the records which you consider would be necessary if such measurement is to be possible.

All calculations are to be displayed to two places of decimals.

Helping hand. The fictitious letter below (pages 45 to 46) includes a Notice under Section 1 of the Statistics of Trade Act 1947 of a type sent out by the Office for National Statistics (ONS).

A compulsory inquiry conducted by
the Government Statistical Service

IN CONFIDENCE

Office for National Statistics

Office for National Statistics
Newport, Gwent NP9 1XG

Grady's Tutorial College
Attn Kim Harvey
Grady House
295 Edgerton Road
London
NW5 7XR

Our ref TI6/7704240000 72/112
Please give this reference number if you contact us

Please correct any errors in name, address or postcode   **26 March 20X4**

Quarterly inquiries into turnover of the distributive and service trades

FIRST QUARTER 20X4 (1 JAN 20X4 TO 31 MARCH 20X4)

Notice under Section 1 of the Statistics of Trade Act 1947

Dear Contributor

Every quarter we send out this inquiry to obtain up-to-date statistics about the distributive and service trades. All larger businesses and a sample of smaller ones are included. Your business has been included in the inquiry.

Your figures will be used with those from other businesses to provide government with information about developments in the distributive and service trades and in the economy. Together with other information, this is an essential part of economic forecasting and policy making.

The inquiry results contribute to quarterly estimates of Gross Domestic Product which are published in an ONS press notice and in other ONS publications.

Because of the importance of the information, this is a statutory inquiry. *Under the Act of 1947, it is compulsory for you to provide the information. This should be returned within three weeks of the end of the period which it covers.* The information you provide will be treated as strictly confidential as required by the Act. I can assure you that it will not be revealed in published statistics in a way which would allow anybody to identify your business or be given to any unauthorised person without your permission.

To save you time, we have made the form as short as possible. There are notes to help you but if you have any difficulties or need more information, my staff on the telephone number shown above will be pleased to assist. If exact figures are not available, informed estimates will do. If you need additional copies of the form, please let us know.

Please accept my thanks for your co-operation. Without this we could not provide a good service to government.

Yours sincerely,

Official use only	
Rec only	
Receipted	
Data pre T/O	
On line T/O	
P/A	

Business Statistics Division

IMPORTANT

Please read the notes before you fill in this form. Give the best estimates you can if you do not have exact figures.

FV			
T16/7704240000 2/112			

1. **Details of business**

   Your business is classified as being in the industry described briefly in the letter accompanying this form. If you think this is wrong, please give a full description of your business. If you are involved in two or more activities, please describe the main one.

2. **Period**

   Period for which you have filled in the form

	Day	Month	Year	
from	/	/		11
to	/	/		12

3. **Turnover** to the nearest £thousand (not including VAT) Total turnover (including fees receivable)

	40

4. **Employees**

   Number of persons employed by the business at the end of the period covered by this return.

   4.1   Total employees

	50

   of which:

4.2	Full-time male	51
4.3	Part-time male	52
4.4	Full-time female	53
4.5	Part-time female	54

5. **Other businesses included in this form**

   The form should be completed for the business named in the covering letter. If, exceptionally, you are unable to limit your return to the activities of this business, please list below the names and VAT registration numbers of the other businesses included.

   Name of business   VAT registration number

   ....
   ....

   (Please continue on a separate sheet if necessary)

   REMARKS: If you have given any information which is significantly different from the last quarter, please explain.

   ....
   ....

PLEASE USE BLOCK CAPITALS

Name of person we should contact if necessary:

Position in business: Date:

Telephone no./ext: Fax/Telex:

NOTES ON FILLING IN THIS FORM

Quarterly inquiries into turnover of the distributive and service trades.

Period

Your return should cover the three months shown on the front of the form. If you do not have figures for that period, the return may be made for the nearest period of a similar length as long as it relates mainly to the one specified. It is important that there are no gaps or overlaps with this period and the period covered by any previous returns that you have made to this inquiry.

Turnover

Give the total amount receivable by the business for services provided or goods sold during the period covered by the form. These amounts should not include VAT. Do not include any amounts receivable from selling or transferring capital assets. The figure given should be for services or goods which you have invoiced rather than cash which you have received, unless a figure for invoiced amounts is not readily available. It is important that the figure is given on a consistent basis from quarter to quarter. Show it to the nearest £ thousand. For example £27,025 should be shown as 27.

Scope of the inquiry

Your turnover should include any business activities carried out within the United Kingdom, (that is England, Scotland, Wales and Northern Ireland). This should include work done in connection with overseas contracts or activities for which invoices are issued by you in the United Kingdom.

Employees

Include full-time and part-time employees (part-time means those who normally work 30 hours a week or less); temporary and casual workers; those off sick, on holiday or on short-term; youth training scheme trainees who have a contract of employment and employment trainees on continuation training; employees who work away from the workplace such as sales reps and lorry drivers.

Exclude those employed by outside contractors or agencies, working proprietors, partners, self-employed, directors not on contract; youth training scheme or employment training trainees without a contract of employment; home workers on piecework rates; former employees still on payroll as pensioners; those who normally work at another establishment such as temporary transfers and secondments.

Helping hand. Like the letter on pages 44 to 46, this fictitious letter (pages 47 to 49) includes an official Notice the same as one used by the ONS. The notes on page 49 do not include all of the notes which the ONS includes with its inquiry form.

Office for National Statistics

A compulsory inquiry conducted by
the Government Statistical Service

IN CONFIDENCE   NEWPORT Gwent NP9 1XG

Ref: QC/17/8100/7104420000/721

GRADY'S TUTORIAL COLLEGE
GRADY HOUSE
249 EDGERTON ROAD
LONDON
NW5 7XR

17 March 20X4

Please correct any errors in name or address

QUARTERLY INQUIRY INTO CAPITAL EXPENDITURE

FIRST QUARTER 20X4 (1 Jan 20X4 to 31 March 20X4)

Notice under Section 1 of the Statistics of Trade Act 1947

Dear Contributor

We conduct this inquiry to obtain up to date information on capital expenditure. The results provide government with essential information for the national accounts and make an important contribution to monitoring the economy. The number of forms is kept to the minimum required to produce reliable results.

Under the above Act, it is necessary for you to provide us with the information requested overleaf. This will be treated as strictly confidential as required by the Act. It will not be revealed in published statistics in a way which would enable your company to be identified, or disclosed to any unauthorised person without your consent.

Please return your completed form by the date shown on the next page of this letter. If exact figures are not readily available, informed estimates are acceptable.

I enclose notes to help you complete the form. In particular, please see the note dealing with the scope of the inquiry. If you have any difficulties in providing data, or on any other point, please contact A.......L...... on 0123 45678.

Thank you for your co-operation.

Yours sincerely

Business Statistics Division
Production Census and Capital Expenditure Branch

PLEASE COMPLETE AND RETURN THIS FORM BY 14 APRIL 20X4

FV	93	Q1
8100/7104420000		

IMPORTANT Please read the enclosed notes before completing this form. If you do not have precise figures available give the best estimates you can. All values should be shown to the nearest £ thousand

1. PERIOD (see note 1

Period covered by the return

		Day	Month	Year
from	08		/	/
to	09		/	/

2. LAND AND BUILDINGS (see note 2)   **£ thousand**

2.1 New building work or other constructional work of a capital nature (excluding the cost of land and of new dwellings)	10	
2.2 Acquisition of land and of existing buildings	20	
2.3 Proceeds of land and buildings disposed of	30	

3. VEHICLES (see note 3)

3.1 New and second-hand acquisitions	40	
3.2 Proceeds of vehicles disposed of	50	

4. PLANT, MACHINERY etc (see note 4)

4.1 New and second-hand acquisitions	60	
4.2 Proceeds of plant, machinery etc disposed of	70	

5. TOTAL

5.1 Total acquisitions (2.1 + 2.2 + 3.1 + 4.1)	90	
5.2 Total disposals (2.3 + 3.2 + 4.2)	100	

6. FINANCE LEASING

6.1 Total amount included in acquisitions at 2.1, 3.1 and 4.1 for assets leased under finance leasing arrangements.	80	

7. COMMENTS ON UNUSUAL FLUCTUATIONS IN FIGURES WOULD BE APPRECIATED

....

Name of person to be contacted if
     necessary...
BLOCK CAPITALS PLEASE

Position in company..................................... Signature.....................................

Telephone No/Ext................................. Fax...........................
                                          Date...........................

Office for National Statistics

NEWPORT Gwent NP9 1XG

QUARTERLY INQUIRY INTO CAPITAL EXPENDITURE
PLEASE READ THESE NOTES BEFORE COMPLETING YOUR RETURN
SCOPE OF THE INQUIRY

This inquiry covers businesses which operate in the United Kingdom. The business is the individual company, partnership, sole proprietorship etc, to which the form has been sent. Figures for subsidiaries of the business addressed should be excluded. In particular, where the business addressed is a holding company figures are required only in respect of the holding company and not for the group as a whole.

NOTES ON INDIVIDUAL QUESTIONS

1. PERIOD

You should enter the start and end dates of the period covered by your return. This should be the calendar quarter specified on the front of the form, or the nearest period of similar length for which figures are available. Where the period is not the calendar quarter, the start date should be no earlier than 20 November 20X3. The total length of the period should not be less than 12 weeks nor more than 16 weeks.

CAPITAL EXPENDITURE

The amounts entered should generally reflect all acquisitions and disposals charged to capital account during the period, together with any other amounts which are regarded as capital items for taxation purposes.

All figures should exclude valued added tax, except that the non-deductible value added tax and Customs and Excise tax paid on passenger cars should be included. Do not deduct any amounts received in grants and/or allowances from government sources, statutory bodies or local authorities.

Expenditure indirectly associated with the acquisition of capital goods, such as the cost of arranging bank loans and servicing them, should be excluded.

If the capital expenditure of the business is nil or very small, a form should be competed to this effect.

2. LAND AND BUILDINGS

New building work (2.1)

Include expenditure on the construction of new building works (other than dwellings) contracted by you whether directly with the constructors or arranged via property developers. Also covered here is expenditure on the associated architects' and surveyors' fees and any legal charges, stamp duties, agents' commissions, etc. Any expenditure undertaken by you when acting as a property developer contracted to carry out the building work by a third party should be excluded.

New building work covers the construction of new buildings, and extensions and improvements to old buildings (including fixtures such as lifts, heating and ventilation systems). The cost of site preparation and other civil engineering work should be included but the cost of land should be recorded against question 2.2

Land and existing buildings (2.2 and 2.3)

Against question 2.2 include all expenditure on land and existing buildings. Land purchase in connection with new building work should also be recorded here and should be estimated where precise figures are not known.

Amounts shown should include the capital cost of freeholds and leaseholds purchased and any leasehold premiums paid. Also covered are architect's and surveyor's fees and any legal charges, stamp duties, agent's commissions, etc associated with these transactions.

Under disposals of land and existing buildings (question 2.3) enter the net amount received after deduction of all transfer costs.

3. VEHICLES (3.1 and 3.2)

These questions cover motor vehicles, ships, aircraft, and railway rolling stock etc.

4. PLANT, MACHINERY AND OTHER CAPITAL EQUIPMENT (4.1 and 4.2)

These questions cover plant, machinery and all other capital equipment (eg computer equipment, office machinery, furniture, mechanical handling equipment and mobile powered equipment such as earth movers, excavators, levellers, mobile cranes).

Practice devolved assessment
2   Iris Ltd

Performance criteria

The following performance criteria are covered in this Practice devolved assessment.

Element 7.3: Prepare VAT returns

1   VAT returns are correctly completed using data from the appropriate recording systems and are submitted within the statutory time limits.

2   Relevant inputs and outputs are correctly identified and calculated.

3   Submissions are made in accordance with current legislation.

4   Guidance is sought from the VAT office when required, in a professional manner.

BPP
PUBLISHING

Practice devolved assessment 2   Iris Ltd

Instructions

This Assessment is designed to test your ability to prepare VAT returns.

You are provided with data (pages 53 to 55) which you must use to complete the tasks listed on page 55.

You are allowed two hours to complete your work.

A high level of accuracy is required. Check your work carefully.

Correcting fluid may be used but should be used in moderation. Errors should be crossed out neatly and clearly. You should write in black ink, not pencil.

A full answer to this Assessment is provided on page 130. Do not turn to the suggested answer until you have completed all parts of the Assessment.

IRIS LTD

THE SITUATION

You are the recently appointed accountant at Iris Ltd. You are about to prepare the company's VAT return for the three months ended 31 December 20X5. You have the following documents to help you.

SALES REPORT		
Month	*Sales*	*VAT*
	£	£
October 20X5	327,190.00	40,545.75
November 20X5	458,429.00	63,486.50
December 20X5	259,361.00	31,608.50

PURCHASES REPORT		
Month	*Purchases*	*VAT*
	£	£
October 20X5	210,630.00	22,863.40
November 20X5	296,539.00	32,805.85
December 20X5	137,784.00	16,894.15

MEMORANDUM

To: Accountant
From: Sales Director
Date: 7 January 20X6
Subject: VAT returns

I can provide my usual confirmation that we have done no business (sales or purchases) outside the UK in the quarter just ended and that we have had no dealings in zero rated goods or services. All our exempt sales were of services. All exempt purchases were attributable to exempt sales. 20% of standard rated purchases were directly attributable to exempt sales, and 45% to standard rated sales.

MEMORANDUM

To: Accountant
From: Warehouse Manager
Date: 13 January 20X6
Subject: Invoicing

I have noticed that in the past month, your department has been working a bit too fast. Goods worth £16,000 (plus VAT) were invoiced before the end of the year, even though they were still in the warehouse when we did our stockcount on 2 January. Won't the customers object to being billed so early? I suppose it's still better for us than the incident three months ago, when goods worth £24,600 (plus VAT) were delivered to the customer on 29 September but not invoiced until 10 October.

MEMORANDUM

To: Accountant
From: Data Processing Manager
Date: 20 January 20X6
Subject: Sales and purchases reports

You telephoned my secretary yesterday and asked a couple of questions about the reports produced by our computerised accounting system. The answers are as follows.

(a)   Sales and purchases are shown net of VAT.

(b)   Any sale of goods is recorded in the system on the day the goods leave the warehouse. This is because we work from the despatch notes. I know that for VAT purposes you always use the date of invoicing, but your predecessor (who left in November) said that she made adjustments on the rare occasions when the invoice did not go out on the same day. We never adjusted our figures to take her adjustments into account. Any sale of services is recorded on the day of invoicing.

MEMORANDUM

To: Accountant
From: Credit Controller
Date: 23 January 20X6
Subject: Bad debts

In March 20X5, we made sales of goods to a customer of £7,600 plus VAT. Payment for the goods was due by 30 April 20X5. We received a cheque for £3,000 in August, but the customer went into liquidation in October. I have now heard that creditors will be paid 40p for every pound they are owed. I have written off the balance of the debt, which will not be paid.

MEMORANDUM

To: Accountant
From: Senior Accountant
Date: 23 January 20X6
Subject: VAT treatment of conference costs

A quote for the cost of the Birmingham conference arrived today. The conference, which is basically a vehicle to promote the company's name and products, will be held next month and is a forum for our sales team to meet interested potential customers as well as our suppliers.

The quotation covers room hire, projection equipment hire (to allow promotional films to be shown) and lunch-time food and drink for all delegates. The conference will run from 11am to 4 pm. The VAT element is over £3,000.

Can you draft a letter to HM Customs & Excise asking whether this VAT is recoverable?

MEMORANDUM

To: Accountant
From: Finance Director
Date: 28 January 20X6
Subject: Mistakes in VAT returns

A friend of mine runs a small business, and he has a query about his VAT. I wouldn't normally trouble you with things which don't concern Iris Ltd directly, but it's probably very simple so I hope you won't mind answering it. He isn't very good at accounts, and is very concerned that he might put the wrong figures on his VAT returns. He wants to know:

(a)   can he just put right any underpayment or overpayment on a later return;

(b)   could he be made to pay a penalty if he makes a mistake?

MEMORANDUM

To: Accountant
From: Data Processing Manager
Date: 28 January 20X6
Subject: New accounting software

We may soon be changing our software. One issue which has come up is that of rounding . The computer could work out amounts of VAT to the nearest hundreth of a penny, but all our invoices will of course have to be in whole pounds and pennies. So that our software is correctly designed, could you remind me of the rules on rounding amounts of VAT?

Tasks

1   Complete Iris Ltd's VAT return for the period.

2   Reply to the Senior Accountant's memorandum.

3   Reply to the finance director's memorandum.

4   Reply to the second memorandum from the data processing manager.

A blank VAT return is provided below.

Value Added Tax Return

For the period
01 10 X5 to 31 12 X5

For Official Use

Registration number | Period
653 5306 77 | 12 X5

You could be liable to a financial penalty if your completed return and all the VAT payable are not received by the due date.

Due date: 31 01 X6

For Official Use

IRIS LTD
1 FLOWER STREET
BLOOMTOWN
BL1 4LN

Your VAT Office telephone number is 0123-4567

ATTENTION

If this return and any tax due are not received by the due date you may be liable to a surcharge.

If you make supplies of goods to another EC Member State you are required to complete an EC Sales List (VAT 101).

Before you fill in this form please read the notes on the back and the VAT Leaflet *"Filling in your VAT return"*.
Fill in all boxes clearly in ink, and write 'none' where necessary. Don't put a dash or leave any box blank. If there are no pence write "00" in the pence column. Do not enter more than one amount in any box.

For official use			£	p
	VAT due in this period on sales and other outputs	1		
	VAT due in this period on acquisitions from other EC Member States	2		
	Total VAT due (the sum of boxes 1 and 2)	3		
	VAT reclaimed in this period on purchases and other inputs (including acquisitions from the EC)	4		
	Net VAT to be paid to Customs or reclaimed by you (Difference between boxes 3 and 4)	5		
	Total value of sales and all other outputs excluding any VAT. Include your box 8 figure	6		00
	Total value of purchases and all other inputs excluding any VAT. Include your box 9 figure	7		00
	Total value of all supplies of goods and related services, excluding any VAT, to other EC Member States	8		00
	Total value of all acquisitions of goods and related services, excluding any VAT, from other EC Member States	9		00

If you are enclosing a payment please tick this box.	DECLARATION: You, or someone on your behalf, must sign below. I, ... declare that the (Full name of signatory in BLOCK LETTERS) information given above is true and complete. Signature.. Date .... 20 A false declaration can result in prosecution.

Trial run devolved assessment

Myllton Ltd

58

Trial run devolved assessment Myllton Ltd

Performance criteria

The following performance criteria are covered in this Trial run devolved assessment.

Element 7.1: Prepare and present periodic performance reports

1 Information derived from different units of the organisation is consolidated into the appropriate form.

2 Information derived from different information systems within the organisation is correctly reconciled.

3 When comparing results over time an appropriate method which allows for changing price levels is used.

4 Transactions between separate units of the organisation are accounted for in accordance with the organisation's procedures.

5 Ratios and performance indicators are accurately calculated in accordance with the organisation's procedures.

6 Reports are prepared in the appropriate form and presented to management within required timescales.

Element 7.2: Prepare reports and returns for outside agencies

1 Relevant information is identified, collated and presented in accordance with the conventions and definitions used by outside agencies.

2 Calculations of ratios and performance indicators are accurate.

3 Authorisation for the despatch of completed reports and returns is sought from the appropriate person.

4 Reports and returns are presented in accordance with outside agencies' requirements and deadlines.

Element 7.3: Prepare VAT returns

1 VAT returns are correctly completed using data from the appropriate recording systems and are submitted within the statutory time limits.

2 Relevant inputs and outputs are correctly identified and calculated.

3 Submissions are made in accordance with current legislation.

4 Guidance is sought from the VAT office when required, in a professional manner.

Trial run devolved assessment Myllton Ltd

Instructions

This Assessment is designed to test your ability to prepare reports and returns.

The situation is provided on page 61.

The tasks to be completed are set out on pages 61 to 64.

The Assessment contains a large volume of data which you will require in order to complete the tasks.

Your answers should be set out in the answer booklet, on pages 67 to 74, using the answer sheets provided.

You are allowed **three hours** to complete your work.

A high level of accuracy is required.

Correcting fluid may be used, but it should be used in moderation. Errors should be crossed out neatly and clearly. You should write in black ink, not pencil.

The information you require is provided as far as possible in the sequence in which you will need to deal with it. However, you are advised to look quickly through all of the material before you begin. This will help you to familiarise yourself with the situation and the information available.

You are reminded that you should not use any unauthorised material, such as books or notes, during this Assessment.

A full answer to this Assessment is provided on page 137. Do not turn to the suggested answer until you have completed all parts of the Assessment.

MYLLTON LTD

THE SITUATION

Your name is Olivia Tran and you work as the Deputy Accountant at Myllton Ltd, 23 Cavour Road, Bridge Trading Estate, New Sarum SPO 7YT.

Myllton Ltd manufactures timber window and door frames which are sold to the building trade.

Myllton Ltd is an autonomous subsidiary company within the Hexa-Gann Group Plc.

Your immediate superior is James Mbanu, the Company Accountant. James reports to Romy Gurlane, Myllton Ltd's Managing Director.

Myllton Ltd is separately registered for VAT; there is no group registration in force. All sales, which are all to UK customers, are standard-rated. The company's local VAT office is at Roebuck House, 24-28 Bedford Place, Southampton SO15 2DB.

A small part of Myllton Ltd's sales are to Jevonille Ltd, a large builders merchants, which is also part of the Hexa-Gann Group. All the timber used by Myllton Ltd is supplied by Graviner Ltd, another group company.

Myllton Ltd has an efficient production control system and a rapid flow of products through the factory. It is, therefore, unnecessary to carry any significant stocks of materials or finished products.

Production is labour intensive. Myllton operates a standard costing system and output is measured in standard hours.

The financial year end for all Hexa-Gann Group companies is 31 December.

Today's date is Thursday 2 August 2002.

Tasks

1   The transfer price of timber from Graviner Ltd to Myllton Ltd has remained unchanged since 1996.

Romy Gurlane believes that the drop in timber prices since 1996 means that Myllton Ltd has been overcharged by Graviner Ltd. Romy is particularly concerned because the Managing Director's annual bonus is based on the Return on Capital Employed achieved by the company in the financial year.

Set out below are the figures for purchases of timber by Myllton Ltd from Graviner Ltd during 2001, together with the relevant price index.

You are required to use these figures to complete the form on page 67 of the answer booklet.

2001	Invoiced purchases of timber from Graviner Ltd, including VAT £'000	Index of materials purchased by the Wood and Wood Products Industry 1996 =100
January	138	96.9
February	173	96.2
March	147	95.8
April	171	95.8
May	138	95.7
June	232	95.5
July	209	95.2
August	196	95.0
September	274	94.6
October	225	94.3
November	201	94.4
December	183	94.4
Total	2,287	n/a

2   You are required to calculate the total value of timber purchased by Myllton Ltd from Graviner Ltd during 2001 at 2001 prices, excluding VAT.

Use the figures you have obtained in Task 1.

Use the form provided on page 68 of the answer booklet and calculate the figures to the nearest £'000 at each step.

3   The following information has been extracted from Myllton Ltd's annual accounts for 2001 and passed to you for analysis. All figures exclude VAT.

	£'000
Sales	4,264
Timber purchases from Graviner Ltd	1,946
Other material purchases	328
Production labour	739
Production overheads	254
Administration overheads	476
Selling and distribution costs	198
Other non-production costs	57
Fixed assets (net book value)	1,847
Current assets	638
Current liabilities	204

You are required to write a memo to Romy Gurlane showing the effect that Graviner Ltd's use of 1996 values for transfer prices has had on the following ratios.

*   The gross profit percentage for 2001
*   The net profit percentage for 2001
*   The return on capital employed for 2001

You should present the ratios in two columns.

- In column one use the figures contained in the 2001 accounts

- In column two show what the figures would be if the timber purchased from Graviner Ltd was valued at 2001 prices instead of 1996 prices, ie using the figure you calculated in Task 2

4   The Hexa-Gann Group Plc is a member of the Timber and Ancillary Trades Federation (TATF). Myllton Ltd and Graviner Ltd are the only companies within the group whose activities fall within the ambit of the TATF. Consequently, any figures requested by the TATF are provided by combining Myllton Ltd and Graviner Ltd's figures into one return on behalf of the Hexa-Gann Group Plc.

Hexa-Gann Group Plc's membership number is H920/58

Myllton Ltd acts as the reporting point for returns to the TATF.

You are given the following figures, which have been taken from Graviner Ltd's annual accounts for 2001. All these figures are compatible with those for Myllton Ltd contained in Task 3.

	£'000
Sales (including sales to other members of the Hexa-Gann Group)	13,420
Timber purchases (all from outside the Hexa-Gann Group)	7,938
Other material purchases	276
Production labour	1,260
Production overheads	319
Administration overheads	684
Selling and distribution costs	276
Other non-production costs	147

On page 70 in the answer booklet you will find a form sent to Hexa-Gann Group Plc by the TATF. You are required to complete this form by combining the figures for Myllton Ltd provided in Task 3 with those for Graviner Ltd above. You should exclude any inter-group purchases or sales between Myllton Ltd and Graviner Ltd, to avoid double counting. Myllton made no sales to Graviner during 2001.

5   Use the memo form on page 71 of the answer booklet to pass the TATF form that you completed in Task 4 to Nigel Lyte (who is the Company Secretary for the Hexa-Gann Group Plc) seeking his signature and authorisation for its despatch by Special Delivery. You should point out that the due date for the return is near.

6   Set out below are figures relating to production and hours worked in the previous three months. You are required to use these figures to complete the table on page 72 of the answer booklet.

Month 2002	Standard hours produced	Production labour hours worked
March	7,236	7,539
April	6,208	6,514
May	6,836	7,258
June	6,871	6,943
July	7,633	7,429

7 You are required to complete the VAT return on page 73 of the answer booklet for Myllton Ltd in respect of the quarter ended 31 July 2002. You have obtained the following information.

Period - 1 May 2002 to 31 July 2002	Excluding VAT £	VAT £
Sales, all to UK customers	1,066,327.67	186,607.34
Purchases from UK suppliers	703,156.21	105,473.43
Purchase of car included above	28,450.90	4,978.90
Acquisitions from other EC member states	13,094.50	2,291.54
VAT bad debt relief being claimed		738.76

Notes.

1. All sales were to UK customers

2. The purchases include some zero rated and exempt supplies

3. The car was purchased for the use of Romy Gurlane. It will be used for private as well as business purposes

4. Payment will be included with the return

5. The return is to be signed by James Mbanu

8 Myllton Ltd has arranged a canal boat trip, to take place on 31 August 2002, for its staff and representatives of its customers. An evening meal will be provided, together with music and a free bar. This is a standard package supplied by Knet Cruises Ltd, who are registered for VAT.

As VAT can only be reclaimed in respect of staff entertainment you are required to draft a letter to your local VAT office seeking advice on the correct treatment of the VAT element of the Knet Cruises invoice.

Use the blank letterhead provided on page 74 of the answer booklet.

Answer booklet for trial run devolved assessment

ANSWER BOOKLET FOR TRIAL RUN DEVOLVED ASSESSMENT 1: MYLLTON LTD

Task 1

Calculation of purchases of timber from Graviner Ltd using 2001 prices.

2001	Monthly purchases at invoiced prices, including VAT £'000	Index of materials purchased by the Wood and Wood Products Industry, 1996 = 100	Value of timber purchases at current prices, including VAT £'000
January	138	96.9	134
February	173	96.2	166
March	147	95.8	141
April	171	95.8	164
May	138	95.7	132
June	232	95.5	222
July	209	95.2	199
August	196	95.0	186
September	274	94.6	259
October	225	94.3	212
November	201	94.4	190
December	183	94.4	173
Total	2,287		2,178

$138 \div 100 \times 96.9$

Notes

1   The first column should contain the monthly invoiced purchases of timber from Graviner Ltd, including VAT, which use transfer prices agreed in 1996.

2   The second column should contain the monthly figures for the Index of prices of materials purchased by the Wood and Wood Products Industry, where 1996 = 100.

3   The third column will contain your calculated value of the invoiced purchases from Graviner Ltd if current prices had been used instead of those set in 1996.

4   Show each monthly purchases figure in column three to the nearest £'000. Your total for column three should be the sum of the monthly figures shown in that column.

Task 2

	£'000
Value of timber purchases at current prices, including VAT	2,178
VAT included above at 17.5%	324
Value of timber purchases at current prices, excluding VAT	1,854

Task 3

MEMO

To:

From:

Subject:

Date:

_____

_____

_____

_____

_____

_____

_____

_____

_____

_____

_____

_____

_____

_____

_____

_____

_____

_____

_____

_____

_____

BPP PUBLISHING

Task 4

Timber and Ancillary Trades Federation

Gloster House, 33 Loville Road, Dartford, Kent DA8 3QQ

TURNOVER AND COSTS RETURN 2000

Company or Business Name	Hexo-Sann Group
Membership number	H920/58
Accounting year end date	31·12·01
Period covered by figures, if less than one year	
	£m
Turnover	15,738
Timber purchases	7,938
Production labour costs	1,999
Other production costs	1,177
Non-production costs	1,838
Total costs	

Notes.
1. All figures should exclude VAT.
2. All figures should be to the nearest £100,000 and expressed as decimal millions (eg £31,832,420 would be £31.8)
3. This return should be signed by an officer of the company, or the owner or a partner if unincorporated.

Signature:	
Name:	
Position:	
Date:	

Please return to Annabelle Peruke at the above address by 6 August 2002, marked 'Private & Confidential'.

Task 5

MEMO

To:

From:

Subject:

Date:

_____

_____

_____

_____

_____

_____

_____

_____

_____

_____

_____

_____

_____

_____

_____

_____

_____

_____

Task 6

MYLLTON LTD

PRODUCTIVITY REPORT

Period	Standard hours produced (3 month total)	Production labour hours worked, (3 month total)	Output hours per input hour
March 02 to May 02	2 0,280	2 1,311	0·952
April 02 to June 02	1 9,715	2 0,715	0·961
May 02 to July 02	2 1,340	2 1,630	0·987

Note. The productivity ratio is to be expressed to three decimal places.

Task 7

Value Added Tax Return
For the period
01 05 02 to 31 07 02

For Official Use

Registration number | Period
578 4060 20 | 07 02

You could be liable to a financial penalty if your completed return and all the VAT payable are not received by the due date.

081 578 4060 19 100 03 98   Q35192

Due date: 31 08 02

James Mbanu
Myllton Ltd
23 Cavour Road
Bridge Trading Estate
New Sarum SP0 7YT   219921/10

For Official Use

Your VAT Office telephone number is 01682-386000

ATTENTION

If this return and any tax due are not received by the due date you may be liable to a surcharge.

If you make supplies of goods to another EC Member State you are required to complete an EC Sales List (VAT 101).

Before you fill in this form please read the notes on the back and the VAT Leaflet *"Filling in your VAT return"*.
Fill in all boxes clearly in ink, and write 'none' where necessary. Don't put a dash or leave any box blank. If there are no pence write "00" in the pence column. Do not enter more than one amount in any box.

	£	p
For official use		
1 VAT due in this period on sales and other outputs	186,607	54
2 VAT due in this period on acquisitions from other EC Member States	2,291	54
3 Total VAT due (the sum of boxes 1 and 2)	188,898	88
4 VAT reclaimed in this period on purchases and other inputs (including acquisitions from the EC)	103 524	83
5 Net VAT to be paid to Customs or reclaimed by you (Difference between boxes 3 and 4)	85,374	05
6 Total value of sales and all other outputs excluding any VAT. Include your box 8 figure	1,066,327	00
7 Total value of purchases and all other inputs excluding any VAT. Include your box 9 figure	716,250	00
8 Total value of all supplies of goods and related services, excluding any VAT, to other EC Member States		00
9 Total value of all acquisitions of goods and related services, excluding any VAT, from other EC Member States	13,094	00

If you are enclosing a payment please tick this box.

DECLARATION: You, or someone on your behalf, must sign below.
I, ... declare that the
(Full name of signatory in BLOCK LETTERS)
information given above is true and complete.

Signature.................................... Date 20

A false declaration can result in prosecution.

F

0196929   IB (October 2000)

VAT 100 (Half)

BPP PUBLISHING

Task 8

MYLLTON LTD

23 Cavour Road, Bridge Trading Estate, New Sarum SP0 7YT
Telephone 01722-883567

_____

_____

_____

_____

_____

_____

_____

_____

_____

_____

_____

_____

_____

_____

_____

_____

_____

_____

_____

Registered office: 23 Cavour Road, Bridge Trading Estate, New Sarum SP0 7YT
Registered in England, number 2314562

AAT Sample simulation

Performance criteria

The following performance criteria are covered in this Simulation.

Element 7.1: Prepare and present periodic performance reports

1 Information derived from different units of the organisation is consolidated into the appropriate form.

2 Information derived from different information systems within the organisation is correctly reconciled.

3 When comparing results over time an appropriate method which allows for changing price levels is used.

4 Transactions between separate units of the organisation are accounted for in accordance with the organisation's procedures.

5 Ratios and performance indicators are accurately calculated in accordance with the organisation's procedures.

6 Reports are prepared in the appropriate form and presented to management within required timescales.

Element 7.2: Prepare reports and returns for outside agencies

1 Relevant information is identified, collated and presented in accordance with the conventions and definitions used by outside agencies.

2 Calculations of ratios and performance indicators are accurate.

3 Authorisation for the despatch of completed reports and returns is sought from the appropriate person.

4 Reports and returns are presented in accordance with outside agencies' requirements and deadlines.

Element 7.3: Prepare VAT returns

1 VAT returns are correctly completed using data from the appropriate recording systems and are submitted within the statutory time limits.

2 Relevant inputs and outputs are correctly identified and calculated.

3 Submissions are made in accordance with current legislation.

4 Guidance is sought from the VAT office when required, in a professional manner.

AAT Sample Simulation Hoddle Ltd

Instructions

This simulation is designed to test your ability to prepare reports and returns.

The simulation contains a large volume of data which you will require in order to complete the tasks. The information you require is provided as far as possible in the sequence in which you will need to deal with it. However, you are advised to look quickly through all of the material before you begin. This will help you to familiarise yourself with the situation and the information available.

Your answers should be set out in the **answer booklet** on pages 89 to 97 using the answer sheets provided.

You are allowed **three hours** to complete your work, although up to 30 minutes extra time may be allowed.

A high level of accuracy is required. Check your work before handing it in.

Correcting fluid may be used but it should be used in moderation. Errors should be crossed out neatly and clearly. You should write in black ink, not pencil.

You are reminded that you should not bring any unauthorised material, such as books or notes, into the simulation. If you have any such material in your possession, you should surrender it to the assessor immediately.

Any instances of misconduct will be brought to the attention the AAT, and disciplinary action may be taken.

A full answer to this simulation is provided on page 147.

HODDLE LTD

THE SITUATION

Your name is Sol Bellcamp and you work as an accounts assistant for a printing company, Hoddle Limited. Hoddle Limited is owned 100 per cent by anther printing company, Kelly Limited. You report to the Group Accountant, Sherry Teddingham.

Hoddle Limited manufactures a wide range of printed materials such as cards, brochures and booklets. Most customers are based in the UK, but sales are also made to other countries in the European Union (EU). There are no exports to countries outside the EU. All of the company's purchases come from businesses within the UK.

Hoddle Limited is registered for VAT and it makes both standard-rated and zero-rated supplies to its UK customers. All sales to other EU countries qualify as zero-rated. The company's local VAT office is at Brendon House, 14 Abbey Street, Pexley PY2 3WR.

Kelly Limited is separately registered for VAT; there is no group registration in force. Both companies have an accounting year ending on 31 March. There are no other companies in the Kelly group.

Hoddle Limited is a relatively small company and sometimes suffers from shortage of capacity to complete customers' jobs. In these cases, the printing work is done by Kelly Limited. Kelly then sells the completed product to Hoddle for onward sale to the customer. The sale from Kelly to Hoddle is recorded in the books of each company at cost; Kelly does not charge a profit margin.

In this simulation you are concerned with the accounting year ended 31 March 2002.

- To begin with you will be required to prepare the VAT return for Hoddle Limited in respect of the quarter ended 31 March 2002.

- You will then be required to prepare certain reports, both for internal use and for an external interfirm comparison scheme, covering the whole accounting year ended 31 March 2002. These reports will treat the two companies as a single group; they will contain consolidated figures, not figures for either of the two companies separately.

Today's date is 9 April 2002.

Space for your answers is provided on pages 89 to 97.

Tasks

1 Refer to the documents on pages 80 and 81, which have been received from Hoddle Ltd's suppliers during March 2002. No entries have yet been made in Hoddle Ltd's books of account in respect of these documents. You are required to explain how you will treat each one of these documents when preparing Hoddle Ltd's VAT return for the period January to March 2002. Use page 89 for your answer.

2 Refer to the sales day book summary, purchases day book summary, cash book summary and petty cash book summary on page 82. These have been printed out from Hoddle Ltd's computerised accounting system for the period January to March 2002. (You are reminded that these summaries do not include the documents dealt with in task 1.) Refer also to the memo on page 83. Using this information you

are required to complete the VAT return of Hoddle Ltd for the quarter ended 31 March 2002. A blank VAT return is provided on page 90.

3   The Group Accountant is considering adoption of the cash accounting scheme for VAT. He believes that Hoddle Limited (though not Kelly Limited) might qualify for the scheme. He has asked you to draft a letter to the VAT office, in his name, requesting certain details of the scheme. He is interested in the turnover limit for the scheme, particularly since Hoddle is a member of a group of companies, and in the effect of the scheme on dealing with bad debts. You are required to draft this letter using the blank letterhead on page 91.

4   Refer to the profit and loss account of Kelly Limited on page 84, which covers the period 1 January to 31 March 2002. You are required to prepare a profit and loss account for the same period in which the results of Hoddle and Kelly are consolidated. Enter your answer on the form provided on page 92 as follows:

   •   Enter the results of Kelly in the first column of the form.

   •   Using the information already provided for earlier tasks construct the results of Hoddle Ltd and enter them in the second column. Note that Hoddle Ltd's stock at 1 January 2002 was valued at £14,638, while stock at 31 March 2002 was valued at £16,052.

   •   Make appropriate adjustments in the third column to eliminate the effects of trading between Kelly and Hoddle.

   •   Calculate the consolidated figures and enter them in the fourth column.

5   Refer to the information on pages 85 and 86. Using this, and information already provided for earlier tasks, you are required to prepare a report for the accountant on the group results for the year ended 31 March 2002. Your report should contain the following:

   •   Key ratios: gross profit margin; net profit margin; return on shareholders' capital employed.

   •   Sales revenue for each quarter, both in actual terms and indexed to a common base.

   •   A pie chart showing the proportion of annual (unindexed) sales earned in each quarter.

   Use page 93 to set out your answer. **Note that you are not required to comment on the results for the year, merely to present them according to the instructions above.**

6   You are required to complete the interfirm comparison form on page 94.

7   You are required to prepare a memo to the group accountant enclosing the interfirm comparison form for authorisation before despatch. Use page 96.

Engineering Supplies Limited

Haddlefield Road, Blaysley CG6 6AW
Tel/fax: 01376 44531

Hoddle Limited
22 Formguard Street
Pexley
PY6 32W

SALES INVOICE NO: *2155*

Date: *27 March 2002*

	£
VAT omitted in error from invoice no 2139	
£2,667.30 @ 17.5%	466.77
Total due	466.77

Terms: net 30 days

VAT registration: 318 1827 58

Alpha Stationery

Ainsdale Centre, Mexton EV1 4DF
Telephone 01392 43215

26 March 2002

1 box transparent folders: red

Total including VAT @ 17.5%	14.84
Amount tendered	20.00
Change	5.16

VAT registration 356 7612 33

JAMIESON & CO

Jamieson House, Baines Road, Gresham GM7 2PQ
Telephone: 01677 35567   Fax: 01677 57640

PROFORMA SALES INVOICE

VAT registration: *412 7553 67*

Hoddle Limited
22 Formguard Street
Pexley
PY6 3QW

For professional services in connection with debt collection

	£
Our fees	350.00
VAT	61.25
Total due	411.25

A VAT invoice will be submitted when the total due is paid in full

BPP PUBLISHING

HODDLE LIMITED
SALES DAY BOOK SUMMARY
JANUARY TO MARCH 2002

	January £	*February* £	*March* £	*Total* £
UK: Zero-rated	20,091.12	22,397.00	23,018.55	65,506.67
UK: Standard-rated	15,682.30	12,914.03	15,632.98	44,229.31
Other EU	874.12	4,992.66	5,003.82	10,870.60
VAT	2,744.40	2,259.95	2,735.77	7,740.12
Total	39,391.94	42,563.64	46,391.12	128,346.70

HODDLE LIMITED
PURCHASES DAY BOOK SUMMARY
JANUARY TO MARCH 2002

	January £	*February* £	*March* £	*Total* £
Purchases	14,532.11	20,914.33	15,461.77	*50,908.21
Distribution expenses	4,229.04	3,761.20	5,221.43	13,211.67
Administration expenses	5,123.08	2,871.45	3,681.62	11,676.15
Other expenses	1,231.00	1,154.99	997.65	3,383.64
VAT	4,027.97	4,543.22	4,119.34	12,690.53
Total	29,143.20	33,245.19	29,481.81	91,870.20

*This figure includes £18,271 of purchases from Kelly Ltd.

HODDLE LIMITED
CASH BOOK SUMMARY
JANUARY TO MARCH 2002

	January £	*February* £	*March* £	*Total* £
Payments				
To creditors	12,901.37	15,312.70	18,712.44	46,926.51
To petty cash	601.40	555.08	623.81	1,780.29
Wages/salaries	5,882.18	6,017.98	6,114.31	18,014.47
Total	19,384.95	21,885.76	25,450.56	66,721.27
Receipts				
VAT from Customs & Excise	2,998.01			2,998.01
From customers	29,312.44	34,216.08	36,108.77	99,637.29
Total	32,310.45	34,216.08	36,108.77	102,635.30
Surplus for month	12,925.50	12,330.32	10,658.21	
Balance b/f	−8,712.41	4,213.09	16,543.41	
Balance c/f	4,213.09	16,543.41	27,201.62	

HODDLE LIMITED
PETTY CASH BOOK SUMMARY
JANUARY TO MARCH 2002

	January £	*February* £	*March* £	*Total* £
Payments				
Stationery	213.85	80.12	237.58	531.55
Travel	87.34	76.50	102.70	266.54
Office expenses	213.66	324.08	199.51	737.25
VAT	86.55	74.38	84.02	244.95
Total	601.40	555.08	623.81	1,780.29
Receipts from cash book	601.40	555.08	623.81	1,780.29
Surplus for month	0.00	0.00	0.00	
Balance b/f	200.00	200.00	200.00	
Balance c/f	200.00	200.00	200.00	

MEMO

To: Sol Bellcamp

From: Sherry Teddingham

Date: 6 April 2002

Subject: Bad debt – Batty Limited

As you probably know, we have had great difficulty in persuading the above customer to pay what he owes us. We invoiced him in July 2001 for £420 plus VAT at the standard rate, but he has always disputed the debt and it looks as though we will never recover it. We wrote it off to the bad debt account in March of this year, so you should take this into account when preparing the VAT return for the quarter just ended.

KELLY LIMITED
PROFIT AND LOSS ACCOUNT
FOR THE THREE MONTHS ENDED 31 MARCH 2002

	£	£
Sales to external customers		275,601
Sales to Hoddle Limited at cost		*20,167
Total sales		295,768
Opening stock	28,341	
Purchases	136,095	
	164,436	
Closing stock	31,207	
Cost of sales		133,229
Gross profit		162,539
Wages and salaries	47,918	
Distribution expenses	28,341	
Administration expenses	30,189	
Stationery	2,541	
Travel	2,001	
Office expenses	3,908	
Interest payable	12,017	
Other expenses	11,765	
		138,680
Net profit for the period		23,859

*This figure includes £1,896 in respect of a job completed on 31 March 2002 but not delivered to Hoddle Limited until 1 April 2002. It is not included in Hoddle Ltd's purchases for the period ended 31 March.

KELLY AND HODDLE
CONSOLIDATED BALANCE SHEET AT 31 MARCH 2002

	£	£
Fixed assets at net book value		1,229,348
Current assets		
Stock	49,155	
Trade debtors	223,009	
VAT recoverable	13,451	
Cash at bank and in hand	40,088	
	325,703	
Current liabilities		
Trade creditors	136,531	
Other creditors	11,740	
	148,271	
Net current assets		177,432
Total assets less current liabilities		1,406,780
Long term liability		
Loan repayable in 2006		372,072
		1,034,708
Capital and reserves		
Called up share capital		234,167
Retained profits		800,541
		1,034,708

KELLY AND HODDLE
QUARTERLY CONSOLIDATED PROFIT AND LOSS ACCOUNTS
FOR THE YEAR ENDED 31 MARCH 2002

	1 April 2001- 30 June 2001 £	1 July 2001- 30 September 2001 £	1 October 2001- 31 December 2001 £	1 January 2002- 31 March 2002 £	1 April 2001- 31 March 2002 £
Sales	325,719	275,230	306,321		
Cost of sales	134,861	109,421	121,358		
Gross profit	190,858	165,809	184,963		
Wages and salaries	63,314	61,167	64,412		
Distribution expenses	34,217	30,135	31,221		
Administration expenses	34,765	33,012	36,415		
Stationery	2,981	2,671	3,008		
Travel	1,975	1,876	2,413		
Office expenses	4,412	4,713	3,083		
Interest payable	12,913	12,714	12,432		
Other expenses	10,981	16,421	15,431		
	165,558	162,709	168,415		
Net profit for the period	25,300	3,100	16,548		

Note for candidates: you are advised to complete the above schedule by filling in the figures for the final quarter in the fourth column and totalling the figures to the year in the final column.

MEMO

To: Sol Bellcamp

From: Sherry Teddingham

Subject: Adjusting for the effects of price rises

Date: 2 April 2002

When presenting your quarterly reports on group results please include an item of information additional to that which you normally present. As well as noting sales revenue by quarter, please present quarterly sales revenue adjusted to take account of price rises.

I have identified a suitable index as follows.

First quarter 2000/01 (base period)	231.8
First quarter 2001/02	239.3
Second quarter 2001/02	241.5
Third quarter 2001/02	244.0
Fourth quarter 2001/02	241.8

I will keep you informed of future movements in this index.

Answer booklet for AAT Sample simulation

ANSWER BOOKLET FOR AAT SIMULATION: HODDLE LTD

Task 1

....

....

....

....

....

....

....

....

....

....

....

....

....

....

....

....

....

....

....

....

....

....

....

Task 2

Value Added Tax Return
For the period
01 01 02 to 31 03 02

For Official Use

Registration number | Period
578 4060 19 | 03 02

You could be liable to a financial penalty if your completed return and all the VAT payable are not received by the due date.

Due date: 30 04 02

```
081 578 4060 19 100 03 98     Q35192
```

MR SHERRY TEDDINGHAM
HODDLE LIMITED
22 FORMGUARD STREET
PEXLEY
PY6 3QW   219921/10

Your VAT Office telephone number is 01682-386000

For
Official
Use

ATTENTION

If this return and any tax due are not received by the due date you may be liable to a surcharge.

If you make supplies of goods to another EC Member State you are required to complete an EC Sales List (VAT 101).

Before you fill in this form please read the notes on the back and the VAT Leaflet *"Filling in your VAT return"*. Fill in all boxes clearly in ink, and write 'none' where necessary. Don't put a dash or leave any box blank. If there are no pence write "00" in the pence column. Do not enter more than one amount in any box.

For official use		£	p
	VAT due in this period on sales and other outputs **1**		
	VAT due in this period on acquisitions from other EC Member States **2**		
	Total VAT due (the sum of boxes 1 and 2) **3**		
	VAT reclaimed in this period on purchases and other inputs (including acquisitions from the EC) **4**		
	Net VAT to be paid to Customs or reclaimed by you (Difference between boxes 3 and 4) **5**		
	Total value of sales and all other outputs excluding any VAT. Include your box 8 figure **6**		00
	Total value of purchases and all other inputs excluding any VAT. Include your box 9 figure **7**		00
	Total value of all supplies of goods and related services, excluding any VAT, to other EC Member States **8**		00
	Total value of all acquisitions of goods and related services, excluding any VAT, from other EC Member States **9**		00

If you are enclosing a payment please tick this box.

DECLARATION: You, or someone on your behalf, must sign below.

I,.. declare that the
(Full name of signatory in BLOCK LETTERS)
information given above is true and complete.

Signature.. Date 20

A false declaration can result in prosecution.

F

0196929   IB (October 2000)

VAT 100 (Half)

Task 3

HODDLE LIMITED

22 Formguard Street, Pexley PY6 3QW
Telephone 01682 431 432256

....

....

....

....

....

....

....

....

....

....

....

....

....

....

....

....

....

....

....

....

Registered office: 22 Formguard Street, Pexley PY6 3QW
Registered in England, number 2314561

Task 4

CONSOLIDATED PROFIT AND LOSS ACCOUNT
FOR THE THREE MONTHS ENDED 31 MARCH 2002

	Kelly £	Hoddle £	Adjustments £	Consolidated £
Sales	_____	_____	_____	_____
Opening stock	_____	_____	_____	_____
Purchases				
Closing stock	_____	_____	_____	_____
Cost of sales	_____	_____	_____	_____
	_____	_____	_____	_____
Gross profit	_____	_____	_____	_____
Wages and salaries				
Distribution expenses				
Administration expenses				
Stationery				
Travel				
Office expenses				
Interest payable				
Other expenses	_____	_____	_____	_____
	_____	_____	_____	_____
	_____	_____	_____	_____
Net profit for the period	_____	_____	_____	_____

Task 5

....

....

....

....

....

....

....

....

....

....

....

....

....

....

....

....

....

....

....

....

....

....

....

....

....

Task 6

INTERFIRM COMPARISON (IFC) DATA (extracts)

Name of company...

Year ended...

Data

	£	% of sales	Industry best	Industry average
Sales				
Gross profit			62.1%	57.3%
Net profit			10.4%	5.8%
Fixed assets				
Current assets				
Current liabilities				
Return on capital employed			10.3%	9.0%

Important note

Before completing this form you should read the explanatory notes on page 95.

Task 6

COMPLETING THE IFC DATA FORM

Explanatory notes

Note 1

'Sales means sales to external customers. Inter-company, inter-divisional or inter-branch sales should be excluded.

Note 2

Fixed assets should be stated at net book value.

Note 3

Return on capital employed is net profit before interest charges, divided by the total of fixed assets (stated at net book value) and net current assets.

Task 7

....

....

....

....

....

....

....

....

....

....

....

....

....

....

....

....

....

....

....

....

....

....

....

....

Workings sheet

....

....

....

....

....

....

....

....

....

....

....

....

....

....

....

....

....

....

....

....

....

....

....

....

....

Workings sheet ....

Answers to practice activities

CHAPTER 1: THE ORGANISATION, ACCOUNTING AND REPORTING

1 DISTINGUISH

- By type of activity
- By size of business
- Profit orientated or non-profit orientated
- Legal status and ownership

2 PAYROLL

Internal reports, such as payroll summaries, should only be submitted to cost centre managers when **authorisation to do so** has been given by the payroll manager. Once the payroll reports are ready, you should send a memo to the payroll manager highlighting the fact that the payroll summaries are ready for despatch **subject to their authorisation**.

3 REPORTS

- Debtors age analysis
- Trial balance
- Balance sheet
- Profit and loss account
- Payroll summary

CHAPTER 2: BUSINESS AND ACCOUNTING INFORMATION

4 DATA AND INFORMATION

Data are the raw materials (facts, figures, etc) which become **information** when they are processed so as to have meaning for the person who receives them, leading to action or decision of some kind.

5 INTERNAL SOURCES

- Invoices
- Orders
- Delivery notes
- Job cards

6 COST ACCOUNTING

- Information about product costs and profitability
- Information about departmental costs and profitability
- Cost information to help with pricing decisions
- Budgets and standard costs
- Actual performance and variances between actual and budget
- Information to help with the evaluation of one-off decisions

CHAPTER 3: STATISTICAL INFORMATION

7 STATEMENTS

(a) The fact that air passenger deaths were up by 10% over last year may not represent a deterioration over last year's performance. For example, many more passengers might have flown this year, so that the probability of an individual being killed might actually be lower than last year. In addition, the actual number of crashes may be lower, even though more passengers were killed (because larger aeroplanes crashed).

(b) It does not follow from the decrease in pass rate that a higher standard was expected. It may be that the standard expected remained the same but the quality of exam scripts was lower than previously.

(c) Inflation is a measure of the rate of change of prices. If annual inflation falls from 10% to 5%, for example, the trend of prices is still upwards. Prices are still increasing at a rate of 5% per annum. So the shopper is wrong to expect prices to be falling just because the rate of inflation is falling.

8 DATA

Primary data are data collected especially for the purpose of whatever survey is being conducted.

Secondary data are data which have already been collected elsewhere, for some other purpose, but which can be used or adapted for the survey being conducted.

9 SECONDARY DATA

The main advantage of secondary data is that unlike primary data, they are available cheaply.

CHAPTER 4: PRESENTING INFORMATION: GRAPHS

10 INDEPENDENT VARIABLE

An **independent variable** is a variable whose value affects the value of the dependent variable. On a graph, the **x axis** is used to represent the independent variable.

11 SCATTERGRAPH

A **scattergraph** is a graph which is used to exhibit data, rather than equations which produce simple lines or curves, in order to compare the way in which the variables vary with each other.

12 BLANKS

The **upper quartile** is the value of the item which is 75% of the way through the cumulative frequencies. It is also known as the third quartile.

The **lower quartile** is the value of the item which is 25% of the way through the cumulative frequencies. It is also known as the first quartile.

CHAPTER 5: PRESENTING INFORMATION: TABLES AND CHARTS

13 SIGNIFICANT DIGITS

(a) 2,197.28

(b) 2,197.3

(c) 2,197

14 DECIMAL PLACES

(a) 38.178

(b) 38.18

(c) 38.2

CHAPTER 6: AVERAGES AND TIME SERIES

15 FORMULA

Arithmetic mean of a frequency distribution, $\bar{x} = \dfrac{\sum fx}{n}$ or $\dfrac{\sum fx}{\sum f}$

Σ = Sigma, the sum of

f = frequency

x = value of variable

n = number of items measured

16 AVERAGES

(a) **The mean**

The **arithmetic mean** is the best known and most widely used average. The arithmetic mean of some data is the sum of the data, divided by the number of items in the data. It is widely used because it gives a convenient and readily understood indication of the **general size** of the data, it takes account of **all items of data** and it is **suitable for further mathematical analysis**. On the other hand, its value can be unduly influenced by a few very large or very small items of data.

(b) **The median**

The **median** is the value of the **middle member** of a set of data, once the data have been arranged in either ascending or descending order. It is one sort of average and it has the following properties.

- It is fairly easy to obtain.
- It is not affected very much by extreme values.
- It is not generally suitable for further statistical analysis.

The median may be more useful than the arithmetic mean in certain circumstances, for instance when determining the average salary of the employees in a company. Since a few employees might have very high salaries, the arithmetic mean could be drawn upwards by these, out of the range of salaries earned by most employees. The mean would then not be representative. The median, however, would be the item in the middle of the ranking, which would be within the range of salaries earned by most employees.

(c) **Time series**

A **time series** is simply a **series of values recorded over time**. Examples of a time series are:

(i) Output at a factory each day for the last month

(ii) Monthly sales over the last two years

(iii) The number of people employed by a company each year for the last 20 years

Time series are often shown on a graph, with time always being the independent variable shown along the x axis, and the values at each time shown along the y axis.

The **features** of a time series are normally taken to be:

• A trend
• Cyclical variations
• Seasonal variations
• Random variations

CHAPTER 7: USING INDEX NUMBERS

17 PRICE INDEX

A **price index** is an index which measures the change in the money value of a group of items over a period of time.

18 SALES INDEX

If £35,000 = 100%, then:

$$£42,000 = \frac{42,000}{35,000} \times 100\% = 120\%$$

$$£40,000 = \frac{40,000}{35,000} \times 100\% = 114\%$$

$$£45,000 = \frac{45,000}{35,000} \times 100\% = 129\%$$

$$£50,000 = \frac{50,000}{35,000} \times 100\% = 143\%$$

The table showing sales for the last five years can now be completed, taking 20X5 as the base year.

Year	Sales (£'000)	Index
20X5	35	100
20X6	42	120
20X7	40	114
20X8	45	129
20X9	50	143

19 MACHINE PRICES

To find the percentage increase since year 9, we take the increase as a percentage of the year 9 value. The increase in the index of 18 points between year 9 and year 14 is therefore a percentage increase of $(18/180 \times 100\%) = 10\%$.

CHAPTER 8: WRITING REPORTS AND COMPLETING FORMS

20 FORMS

The code letter (L, H, P, V or T) has been omitted from the tax code at the date of leaving.

CHAPTER 9: REPORTING PERFORMANCE

21 COST CENTRE

A **cost centre** is a location, person or item of equipment for which costs may be ascertained and related to cost units for control purposes.

Examples of cost centres are

- A department
- A machine
- A project
- A new product

22 TRANSFER PRICE

(a) A **transfer price** is the price at which goods or services are transferred from one process or department to another.

(b) A transfer price might be based on the following.

- Marginal cost
- Full cost
- Market price
- Negotiated or discounted price

23 CONSOLIDATION OF INFORMATION

	Dept A		Dept B		Adjust- ment		Total
	£	£	£	£	£	£	£
Sales		720,000		1,080,000 [(1)]	92,000		1,708,000
Cost of sales:							
Opening stock	144,000		180,000			324,000	
Purchases	420,000 [(2)]		648,000		92,000	976,000	
	564,000		828,000			1,300,000	
Less closing stock	156,000		216,000			372,000	
		408,000		612,000			928,000
Gross profit		312,000		468,000			780,000
Less expenses:							
Selling & distribution	91,200		136,800			228,000	
Administration	69,800		105,800			175,600	
Lighting & heating	4,000		19,200			23,200	
Rent & rates	76,000		38,000			114,000	
		241,000		299,800			540,800
Net profit		71,000		168,200			239,200

BPP PUBLISHING

CHAPTER 10: MEASURING PERFORMANCE

24 PRODUCTION AND PRODUCTIVITY

Production is the quantity or volume of output produced. It is the number of units produced, or the actual number of units produced converted into an equivalent number of 'standard hours of production'.

Productivity is the measure of the efficiency with which output has been produced.

25 ROCE

Return on capital employed (ROCE) (also called return on investment, ROI) is calculated as (profit/capital employed) × 100% and shows how much profit has been made in relation to the amount of resources invested.

26 NET PROFIT MARGIN

$$\text{Net profit margin} = \frac{\text{Net profit}}{\text{Turnover}} \times 100\%$$

20X1 $\dfrac{75,000}{600,000} \times 100\% = 12.5\%$

20X2 $\dfrac{80,000}{800,000} \times 100\% = 10\%$

CHAPTER 11: THE VAT CHARGE AND VAT RECORDS

27 JULIE

Helping hand. The total collected by HM Customs & Excise is £1,000 × 7/47% = £148.94, the VAT on the final sale to Jo.

Trader	Working	£	VAT return to	Due date
John's Frantic Furniture Ltd	£600 × 0.175 – £10.50	94.50	31.3.03	30.4.03
M&F plc	£600 × 0.175	(105.00)	31.3.03	*30.4.03
Thomas	£70.50 × 7/47	10.50	31.3.03	30.4.03
M&F plc	£1,000 × 7/47	148.94	30.6.03	31.7.03
		148.94		

*The VAT return with a repayment on it is due by 30.4.03 and the repayment will be made shortly after Custom's receive it.

28 COCO LTD

Helping hand. All the documents in fact meet the requirements of VAT law, but you should have checked that this was so. Input VAT can only be reclaimed if the purchaser holds a valid VAT invoice. If an invoice issued by CoCo Ltd had shown too little VAT, the shortfall would have had to be accounted for.

The total VAT on sales and other outputs (Box 1) is as follows.

	£
Sale to Job Ltd	131.25
Sale to The Dublin company	0.00
Sale to Supplies plc	708.75
	840.00
Less credit to Job Ltd	5.25
	834.75

The Box 2 figure is 'None' so the Box 3 figure is the same as the Box 1 figure.

The total input VAT (Box 4) is as follows.

	£
Purchase from Clay Supplies plc	700.00
Purchase from Glaze Supplies Ltd	486.50
	1,186.50
Less overstatement in previous period	600.00
	586.50

The Box 5 figure is £(834.75 - 586.50) = £248.25. Because a payment will be made, the box to the left of the declaration must be ticked.

The Box 6 figure is £(750.00 + 4,500 + 4,050 - 30.00) = £9,270.00

The Box 7 figure is £(4,000 + 2,780) = £6,780.

The Box 8 figure is £4,500

The Box 9 figure is 'None'.

BPP PUBLISHING

Value Added Tax Return
For the period
01 01 03 to 31 03 03

Registration number	Period
212 7924 36	03 03

You could be liable to a financial penalty if your completed return and all the VAT payable are not received by the due date.

Due date: 30 04 03

For official use	

CoCo LTD
CoCo HOUSE
GOSFORTH
G4 0BB

Your VAT Office telephone number is 0123-4567

ATTENTION

If this return and any tax due are not received by the due date you may be liable to a surcharge.

If you make supplies of goods to another EC Member State you are required to complete an EC Sales List (VAT 101).

Before you fill in this form please read the notes on the back and the VAT Leaflet *"Filling in your VAT return"*. Fill in all boxes clearly in ink, and write 'none' where necessary. Don't put a dash or leave any box blank. If there are no pence write "00" in the pence column. Do not enter more than one amount in any box.

For official use			£	p
	VAT due in this period on sales and other outputs	1	834	75
	VAT due in this period on acquisitions from other EC Member States	2	NONE	
	Total VAT due (the sum of boxes 1 and 2)	3	834	75
	VAT reclaimed in this period on purchases and other inputs (including acquisitions from the EC)	4	586	50
	Net VAT to be paid to Customs or reclaimed by you (Difference between boxes 3 and 4)	5	248	25
	Total value of sales and all other outputs excluding any VAT. Include your box 8 figure	6	9,270	00
	Total value of purchases and all other inputs excluding any VAT. Include your box 9 figure	7	6,780	00
	Total value of all supplies of goods and related services, excluding any VAT, to other EC Member States	8	4,500	00
	Total value of all acquisitions of goods and related services, excluding any VAT, from other EC Member States	9	NONE	00

If you are enclosing a payment please tick this box. ✓

DECLARATION: You, or someone on your behalf, must sign below.

I, ...ANNE ACCOUNTANT.......... declare that the
(Full name of signatory in BLOCK LETTERS)
information given above is true and complete.

Signature.......*A Accountant*....... Date 25 April 2003

A false declaration can result in prosecution.

29 CLIPPER LTD

Helping hand. All the invoices except (d) look superficially plausible, but in fact (d) is the only valid invoice. This shows the importance of attention to detail in applying VAT law.

(a) The invoice from Jupiter plc is invalid because the invoice number has been omitted.

(b) The invoice from Hillside Ltd is invalid because it does not show the supplier's address. In all other respects it meets the requirements for a valid VAT invoice.

(c) The invoice from Generous plc is invalid because the supplier's VAT registration number is not shown and because the type of supply (presumably a sale) is not shown. Finally, the invoice is invalid because the applicable rates of VAT (17.5% and 0%) are not shown.

(d) The total value of the supply by Jewels & Co, including VAT, does not exceed £100, so a less detailed invoice is permissible.

The invoice is valid, because it includes all the information which must be shown on a less detailed invoice.

CHAPTER 12: THE COMPUTATION AND ADMINISTRATION OF VAT

30 ZAG PLC

Helping hand. Because Zag plc makes some exempt supplies, not all the VAT on purchases can be recovered. The VAT on purchases which is not attributable to either taxable supplies or exempt supplies must be apportioned.

(a) Box 1: VAT due on outputs
The figure is £877,500 × 17.5% = £153,562.50

(b) Box 2: VAT due on acquisitions
None.

(c) Box 3: sum of Boxes 1 and 2 = £153,562,50

(d) Box 4: VAT reclaimed on inputs

The figure is as follows.

Apportionment percentage = (877,500 + 462,150)/(877,500 + 462,150 + 327,600) = 80.35%, rounded up to 81%.

	£
Tax on purchases attributable to taxable supplies £585,000 × 17.5%	102,375.00
Tax on unattributable purchases	
£468,000 × 17.5% × 81%	66,339.00
	168,714.00

(e) Box 5: net VAT to be paid or reclaimed

The amount reclaimable is £(168,714 – 153,562.50) = £15,151.50.

Value Added Tax Return

For the period
30 03 03 to 30 06 03

Registration number	Period
483 8611 98	06 03

You could be liable to a financial penalty if your completed return and all the VAT payable are not received by the due date.

Due date: 31 07 03

For official use

ZAG PLC
32 CASE STREET
ZEDTOWN
ZY4 3JN

Your VAT Office telephone number is 0123-4567

ATTENTION

If this return and any tax due are not received by the due date you may be liable to a surcharge.

If you make supplies of goods to another EC Member State you are required to complete an EC Sales List (VAT 101).

Before you fill in this form please read the notes on the back and the VAT Leaflet *"Filling in your VAT return"*.
Fill in all boxes clearly in ink, and write 'none' where necessary. Don't put a dash or leave any box blank. If there are no pence write "00" in the pence column. Do not enter more than one amount in any box.

For official use			£	p
	VAT due in this period on sales and other outputs	1	153,562	50
	VAT due in this period on acquisitions from other EC Member States	2	NONE	
	Total VAT due (the sum of boxes 1 and 2)	3	153,562	50
	VAT reclaimed in this period on purchases and other inputs (including acquisitions from the EC)	4	168,714	00
	Net VAT to be paid to Customs or reclaimed by you (Difference between boxes 3 and 4)	5	15,151	50
	Total value of sales and all other outputs excluding any VAT. Include your box 8 figure	6		00
	Total value of purchases and all other inputs excluding any VAT. Include your box 9 figure	7		00
	Total value of all supplies of goods and related services, excluding any VAT, to other EC Member States	8		00
	Total value of all acquisitions of goods and related services, excluding any VAT, from other EC Member States	9		00

If you are enclosing a payment please tick this box.

DECLARATION: You, or someone on your behalf, must sign below.

I, ... declare that the
(Full name of signatory in BLOCK LETTERS)
information given above is true and complete.

Signature.. Date .... 19 ....
A false declaration can result in prosecution.

31   PAUL LUCAS

Helping hand. You first had to compute the relevant totals, then you had to check the position on partial exemption.

Date cash received	Standard rated turnover £	Zero rated turnover £	Exempt turnover £	VAT at 7/47 £
1.1.03	310.50			46.24
2.1.03	410.75			61.18
5.1.03	719.25			107.12
4.1.03		640.30		
20.1.03		721.50		
1.2.03	400.00			59.57
1.2.03			190.50	
7.2.03		207.50		
7.2.03	300.00			44.68
12.2.03			400.00	
1.3.03			525.50	
2.3.03		275.50		
31.3.03	299.99			44.68
	2,440.49	1,844.80	1,116.00	363.47

Total taxable turnover is £(2,440.49 – 363.47 + 1,844.80) = £3,921.82. Total turnover is £(3,921.82 + 1,116,00) = £5,037.82.

The output VAT in respect of fuel is £422.00 × 7/47 = £62.85, so total output VAT is £(363.47 + 62.85) = £426.32.

The scale charge net of VAT is £(422.00 – 62.85) = £359.15, so the Box 6 figure is £(5,037.82 + 359.15) = £5,396.97, rounded down to £5,396.

Date cash Paid	Purchase £	VAT at 7/47 £
10.1.03	400.00	59.57
4.1.03	527.13	78.51
5.2.03	702.10	
20.2.03	600.00	89.36
1.3.03	212.21	
	2,441.44	227.44

The purchases net of VAT (Box 7) are £(2,441.44 - 227.44) = £2,214.

Input VAT attributable to exempt supplies is 1,116.00/5,396.97 = 20.67%, rounded to 20% (*exempt* percentage *down*) × £227.44 = £45.49. As this is not more than £625 a month on average and not more than half of all input VAT, all input VAT is recoverable.

Value Added Tax Return

For the period

01 01 03 to 31 03 03

Registration number	Period
483 8611 98	03 03

You could be liable to a financial penalty if your completed return and all the VAT payable are not received by the due date.

Due date: 30 04 03

For official use

MR PAUL LUCAS
12 HALDANE ROAD
BRADFORD
BR4 3JN

Your VAT Office telephone number is 0123-4567

ATTENTION

If this return and any tax due are not received by the due date you may be liable to a surcharge.

If you make supplies of goods to another EC Member State you are required to complete an EC Sales List (VAT 101).

Before you fill in this form please read the notes on the back and the VAT Leaflet *"Filling in your VAT return"*.
Fill in all boxes clearly in ink, and write 'none' where necessary. Don't put a dash or leave any box blank. If there are no pence write "00" in the pence column. Do not enter more than one amount in any box.

		£	p
VAT due in this period on sales and other outputs	1	426	32
VAT due in this period on acquisitions from other EC Member States	2	None	
Total VAT due (the sum of boxes 1 and 2)	3	426	32
VAT reclaimed in this period on purchases and other inputs (including acquisitions from the EC)	4	227	44
Net VAT to be paid to Customs or reclaimed by you (Difference between boxes 3 and 4)	5	198	88
Total value of sales and all other outputs excluding any VAT. Include your box 8 figure	6	5,396	00
Total value of purchases and all other inputs excluding any VAT. Include your box 9 figure	7	2,214	00
Total value of all supplies of goods and related services, excluding any VAT, to other EC Member States	8	None	00
Total value of all acquisitions of goods and related services, excluding any VAT, from other EC Member States	9	None	00

For official use

If you are enclosing a payment please tick this box. ✓

DECLARATION: You, or someone on your behalf, must sign below.

I, ... PAUL LUCAS .... declare that the
(Full name of signatory in BLOCK LETTERS)
information given above is true and complete.

Signature.......... *Paul Lucas* .... Date 28 April 2003

A false declaration can result in prosecution.

32   MAYFAIR PLC

Helping hand. The current VAT system for trade with other European Union States is designed so that when goods will be resold by a VAT registered trader in the destination state, that trader will impose the local VAT rate on the final consumer; but where the sale between states is to the final consumer, VAT is charged by the seller at the rate applying in the seller's state.

		£
(a)	Output VAT £1,500 × 17.5%	262.50
(b)	Input VAT £19,250 × 17.5%	(3,368.75)
(c)	Input VAT on taxable acquisition £6,000 × 17.5%	(1,050.00)
(c)	Output VAT on taxable acquisition £6,000 × 17.5%	1,050.00
(d)	Zero rated export	0.00
(e)	Zero rated sale to EU customer	0.00
	Recoverable from HM Customs & Excise	(3,106.25)

GENERAL – PREPARING REPORTS AND RETURNS

33   INCOME STATEMENT

COMMA LIMITED
INCOME STATEMENT

| | September 20X2 | | | | 9 months to September 20X2 | | | |
| | Budget | | Actual | | Budget | | Actual | |
	£m	%	£m	%	£m	%	£m	%
Net sales	2.14	100	2.02	100	22.8	100	23.8	100
Less:								
Standard cost	1.12	52	1.02	50	11.6	51	12.3	52
Variances	0.17	8	0.24	12	1.9	8	2.3	10
Other costs	0.19	9	0.23	11	2.7	12	1.9	8
Inter-company contrib	(0.12)	(6)	(0.18)	(9)	(1.6)	(7)	(1.3)	(5)
Manufacturing margin	0.78	36	0.71	35	8.2	36	8.6	36
Selling expenses	0.21	10	0.18	9	2.5	11	2.6	11
Administrative expenses	0.31	14	0.32	16	3.4	15	3.3	14
Inter-company contrib	(0.04)	(2)	(0.02)	(1)	(0.5)	(2)	(0.2)	(1)
Operating income	0.30	14	0.23	11	2.8	12	2.9	12
Inter-company (net)	(0.02)	(1)	0.02	1	(0.2)	(1)	-	-
Income before tax	0.28	13	0.25	12	2.6	11	2.9	12
Tax	0.15	7	0.10	5	1.4	6	1.4	6
Net income	0.13	6	0.15	7	1.2	5	1.5	6

	Last year		Last year	
Net sales	1.85	100	22.4	100
Manufacturing margin	0.61	33	7.8	35
Operating income	0.21	11	2.2	10

BPP PUBLISHING

34 PIE CHART

Net sales by geographical market 20W6 and 20X1

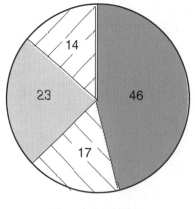 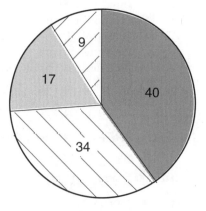

% sales, 20W6   % sales, 20X1

 UK Sales

 EU exports

 North America

 Other

Workings	£'000	*20X1* £'000	%	£'000	*20W6* £'000	%
Home sales		12,249	40		9,273	46
Eire	2,015			-		
Germany	3,605			1,457		
France	2,309			1,200		
Other EU	2,419			894		
EU exports total		10,348	34		3,551	17
Canada	1,722			1,888		
USA	3,402			2,841		
North America		5,124	17		4,729	23
Nigeria	1,521			1,722		
Other non-EU	1,182			1,142		
Other total		2,703	9		2,864	14
		30,424	100		20,417	100

35   BAR CHART

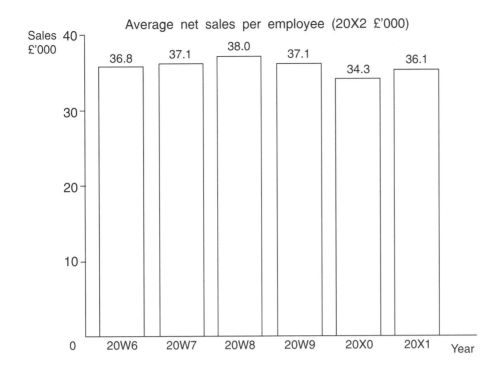

Workings

Total net sales				Current value 20X2	Average e'ees	Sales per e'ee
	£'000			£'000		£'000
20W6	20,418	× 164.9/128.2	=	26,263	713	36.8
20W7	22,084	× 164.9/132.7	=	27,443	739.5	37.1
20W8	23,783	× 164.9/139.5	=	28,113	764	36.8
20W9	25,621	× 164.9/146.2	=	28,898	789	36.6
20X0	28,088	× 164.9/150.7	=	30,735	896.5	34.3
20X1	30,424	× 164.9/157.8	=	31,793	880.5	36.1

BPP PUBLISHING

36   KEY FINANCIAL RATIOS

EMERALD TAXIS LTD
SIX MONTHS ENDED 30 JUNE 20X7

KEY FINANCIAL RATIOS

Vehicle	1 SC84 £	2 SC101 £	3 SC105 £	4 SC126 £	5 SC191 £	6 SC213 £	7 SC220 £	8 SC225 £	Overall £
(a) Income per operating mile	0.90	0.91	0.88	0.92	0.85	0.90	0.91	0.91	0.90
(b) Income per operating hour	8.85	9.53	8.98	9.76	7.56	8.51	9.51	9.70	9.09
(c) Income per operating day	80.11	90.49	76.43	88.95	64.28	76.63	85.56	87.85	81.57
(d) Contribution per operating mile	0.41	0.43	0.40	0.46	0.30	0.39	0.45	0.45	0.42
(e) Contribution per operating hour	4.06	4.55	4.06	4.87	2.65	3.73	4.67	4.80	4.21
(f) Contribution per operating day	36.74	43.21	34.58	44.40	22.53	33.61	42.07	43.47	37.82
(g) Variable cost per operating mile	0.49	0.48	0.48	0.46	0.55	0.51	0.46	0.46	0.48
(h) Variable cost per operating hour	4.79	4.98	4.92	4.89	4.91	4.78	4.83	4.90	4.87
(i) Variable cost per operating day	43.37	47.28	41.86	44.55	41.75	43.02	43.48	44.38	43.75
(j) Fixed cost per operating mile	0.26	0.23	0.25	0.23	0.32	0.25	0.24	0.22	0.25
(k) Fixed cost per operating hour	2.59	2.42	2.60	2.43	2.84	2.37	2.51	2.32	2.50
(l) Fixed cost per operating day	23.43	22.97	22.11	22.19	24.16	21.37	22.58	21.05	22.46
(m) Net profit (loss) per operating mile	0.15	0.20	0.14	0.23	(0.02)	0.14	0.21	0.23	0.17
(n) Net profit (loss) per operating hour	1.47	2.13	1.46	2.44	(0.19)	1.36	2.17	2.47	1.71
(o) Net profit (loss) per operating day	13.31	20.24	12.46	22.21	(1.63)	12.24	19.49	22.42	15.36
(p) Percentage net profit to income	16.6%	22.4%	16.3%	25.0%	(2.5%)	16.0%	22.8%	25.5%	18.8%

37   GRAPH

The total turnover for the period of £115,260 can be analysed into variable costs, fixed costs and net profit as shown below.

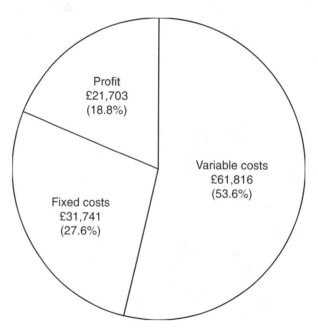

Profit
£21,703
(18.8%)

Variable costs
£61,816
(53.6%)

Fixed costs
£31,741
(27.6%)

Workings

Vehicle	1	2	3	4	5	6	7	8	Total
	£	£	£	£	£	£	£	£	£
Income	14,500	16,289	13,376	16,100	10,285	13,410	15,400	15,900	115,260
Variable costs									
Fuel	1,210	1,561	1,220	1,310	875	1,077	1,185	1,310	9,748
Wages	6,500	6,800	5,960	6,600	5,440	6,300	6,480	6,560	50,640
Tyres	80	85	75	85	65	81	87	90	648
Maintenance	60	65	70	68	300	70	75	72	780
Total variable costs	7,850	8,511	7,325	8,063	6,680	7,528	7,827	8,032	61,816
Contribution	6,650	7,778	6,051	8,037	3,605	5,882	7,573	7,868	53,444
Fixed costs									
Licence	75	75	75	75	75	75	75	75	600
Reg fee	65	65	65	65	65	65	65	65	520
Insurance	610	700	590	620	575	550	610	560	4,815
Depreciation	1,250	1,050	900	1,000	875	800	1,050	850	7,775
Administration	2,180	2,180	2,180	2,180	2,180	2,180	2,180	2,180	17,440
Maintenance	60	64	60	77	95	70	85	80	591
Total fixed costs	4,240	4,134	3,870	4,017	3,865	3,740	4,065	3,810	31,741
Net profit/(loss)	2,410	3,644	2,181	4,020	(260)	2,142	3,508	4,058	21,703

Pie chart workings

	£	%
Variable costs	61,816	53.6
Fixed costs	31,741	27.6
Profit	21,703	18.8
Turnover	115,260	100.0

Helping hand. Alternatively, a bar chart could be presented.

38 TABLE

VEHICLES RANKED BY NET PROFIT/(LOSS) PER OPERATING DAY

Vehicle	£
SC225	22.42
SC126	22.21
SC101	20.24
SC220	19.49
SC84	13.31
SC105	12.46
SC213	12.24
SC191	(1.63)

39 STATEMENT

Average income per operating mile = £0.90

Average variable costs per operating mile = £0.48

Average fixed cost per vehicle £31,741 ÷ 8 × 2 = £7,935 per annum.

BPP PUBLISHING

Projected mileage = 36,500
NEW VEHICLE: ESTIMATED ANNUAL INCOME AND COSTS

	£
Income (36,500 × £0.90)	32,850
Less variable costs (36,500 × £0.48)	(17,520)
Contribution	15,330
Fixed costs	(7,935)
Net profit/(loss)	7,395

40 RPI

Inflation factors

20X2	155.1/139.2 = 1.114
20X3	155.1/141.9 = 1.093
20X4	155.1/146.0 = 1.062
20X5	155.1/150.7 = 1.029
20X6	= 1.000

Turnover

	Actual terms	*Real (20X6) terms*	*Real annual growth %*
	£	£	
20X2	153,640	171,155	-
20X3	167,040	182,575	6.7
20X4	185,600	197,107	8.0
20X5	201,000	206,829	4.9
20X6	215,000	215,000	4.0

41 REAL TERMS

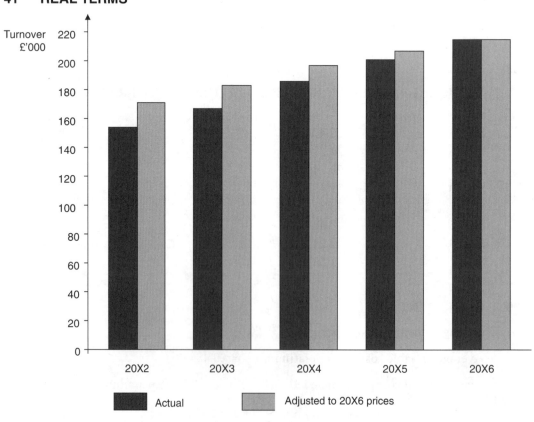

Workings

Turnover	£
April	18,774
May	19,942
June	20,425
	59,141

42 FORMS

NATIONAL TAXI FEDERATION
RETURN FOR SIX MONTHS TO JUNE 20X7
Company name: Emerald Taxis Limited
Membership number: EM002

Performance statistics:	*This period*	*20X6 full year*	*NTF 20X6 average*
Average revenue per vehicle operating day	£81.57	£78.02	£79.70
Average total costs per vehicle operating day	£66.21	£61.07	£60.14
Average revenue per operating mile	£0.90	£0.88	£0.87
Average total costs per operating mile	£0.73	£0.68	£0.67
Net profit as percentage of total revenue	18.8%	17.1%	22.9%
Average mileage per operating day	90.67 miles	88.66 miles	91.84 miles
Average mileage per operating hour	10.10 miles	10.01 miles	9.75 miles

Signed: .... Date: ....

Please submit this form to NTF Head Office as soon as possible.

GENERAL – PREPARING VAT RETURNS

43 ERRORS

Errors

Invoice 573: The amount of VAT due should be £9,100, giving a gross total payable of £61,100.

Invoice 574: The amount of VAT due should be £21,503.44, giving a gross total payable of £144,380.24.

Invoice from Silk Ltd: The invoice is not dated. Secondly a less detailed invoice cannot be issued where the goods supplied exceed £100 value as they do in this case.

44 OUTPUT VAT

Output VAT

	£
Invoice to Bar plc	8,504.68
Invoice to Cormick Ltd (corrected amount shown)	9,100.00
Invoice to Work plc (corrected amount shown)	21,503.44
Invoice to Monet plc	40,722.67
	79,830.79
Less credit note to Sole plc	77.00
	79,753.79
Less error in previous period	2,500.00
	77,253.79

45 INPUT VAT

Input VAT

	£
Invoice from Tarski plc	29,865.50
Invoice from Course Ltd: £83.60 × 7/47	12.45
Invoice from Silk Ltd: no valid VAT invoice	0.00
Call from public telephone	0.89
Car park fee	2.68
	29,881.52
Less credit note from Tarski plc	210.00
	29,671.52
Bad debt relief on debt from Trib Ltd (over six months old)	665.00
	30,336.52
Less error in previous period	1,600.00
	28,736.52

46 NET TURNOVER

	£
Invoice to Bar plc	49,590.00
Invoice to Cormick Ltd	52,000.00
Invoice to Work plc	122,876.80
Invoice to Monet plc	237,450.00
	461,916.80
Less credit note to Sole plc	440.00
Total net turnover	461,476.80

47 NET PURCHASES

	£
Invoice from Tarski plc	170,660.00
Invoice from Course Ltd £83.60 × 40/47	71.15
Invoice from Silk Ltd £270.25 × 40/47	230.00
Expenses	345.97
	171,307.12
Less credit note from Tarski plc	1,200.00
Total net purchases	170,107.12

48 NET ERROR

The net error is £(2,500 − 1,600) = £900, which is not over £2,000 so it may be corrected on the return.

49 VAT ACCOUNT

TONK PLC

VAT ACCOUNT FOR THE VAT PERIOD FROM SEPTEMBER TO
NOVEMBER 20X7

VAT allowable	£	VAT payable	£
Input VAT allowable		Output VAT due	79,830.79
£(29,881.52 - 210.00)	29,671.52	Adjustment for credit	
Correction of error	(1,600.00)	allowed	(77.00)
Refunds for bad debts	665.00	Correction of error	(2,500.00)
	28,736.52		
Cash (payment to HM			77,253.79
Customs & Excise)	48,517.27		
	77,253.79		77,253.79

50   VAT RETURN

Value Added Tax Return
For the period
01 09 X7 to 30 11 X7

For Official Use

Registration number | Period

154 9131 32 | 11X7

You could be liable to a financial penalty if your completed return and all the VAT payable are not received by the due date.

Due date: 31 12 X7

For Official Use

ATTENTION

If this return and any tax due are not received by the due date you may be liable to a surcharge.

If you make supplies of goods to another EC Member State you are required to complete an EC Sales List (VAT 101).

TONK PLC
1 PLINK LANE
INFERTOWN
IN2 4DA

If you have a general enquiry or need advice please call our National Advice Service on 0845 010 9000

Before you fill in this form please read the notes on the back and the VAT Leaflet *"Filling in your VAT return"*.
Fill in all boxes clearly in ink, and write 'none' where necessary. Don't put a dash or leave any box blank. If there are no pence write "00" in the pence column. Do not enter more than one amount in any box.

For official use			£	p
VAT due in this period on sales and other outputs	1		77,253	79
VAT due in this period on acquisitions from other EC Member States	2		NONE	
Total VAT due (the sum of boxes 1 and 2)	3		77,253	79
VAT reclaimed in this period on purchases and other inputs (including acquisitions from the EC)	4		28,736	52
Net VAT to be paid to Customs or reclaimed by you (Difference between boxes 3 and 4)	5		48,517	27
Total value of sales and all other outputs excluding any VAT. Include your box 8 figure	6		461,476	00
Total value of purchases and all other inputs excluding any VAT. Include your box 9 figure	7		170,107	00
Total value of all supplies of goods and related services, excluding any VAT, to other EC Member States	8		NONE	00
Total value of all acquisitions of goods and related services, excluding any VAT, from other EC Member States	9		NONE	00

If you are enclosing a payment please tick this box. ✓

DECLARATION: You, or someone on your behalf, must sign below.
I, **PETRA SMITH** declare that the
(Full name of signatory in BLOCK LETTERS)
information given above is true and complete.
Signature *P Smith*   Date *15/12 20X7*
A false declaration can result in prosecution.

51   DATE

The VAT return and the cash payment due must be delivered to HM Customs & Excise by the end of the month following the end of the VAT return period. So for this return the due date is 31 December 20X7.

Answers to practice devolved assessments

ANSWERS TO PRACTICE DEVOLVED ASSESSMENT 1: GRADY'S TUTORIAL COLLEGE

Helping hand. Not many figures need to be entered on the ONS forms. However, the forms have quite lengthy accompanying notes. This highlights an important skill when completing reports and returns: to be able to review the information available in full and to select the information which is relevant to the task.

Task 1

See the completed forms on pages 126 and 127.

Working

Total turnover is calculated as follows.

	£	£
College Division		
YTD 31.3.X4	583,636	
YTD 31.12.X3	(422,629)	
		161,007
Bookshop		
YTD 31.3.X4	71,094	
YTD 31.12.X3	(46,931)	
		24,163
Interdivisional (394 + 481 + 192)		(1,067)
		184,103

Task 2

The return for the *Quarterly inquiry into turnover*, as stated in the ONS letter, should be returned within three weeks of the end of the period to which it relates. This period ends on 31 March 20X4 and so the form should be returned by 21 April 20X4.

The return for the *Quarterly inquiry into capital expenditure* should be returned by 14 April 20X4, as stated at the top of the form.

In view of these dates, neither form can wait for Kim's return from holiday and I would therefore take the following action.

(a) Remind Kim of the dates by which the returns must be made and request that she be available to sign them before she leaves at 5.30 pm this evening.

(b) Make arrangements to complete the forms for signature today. The forms should be drafted by 4 pm at the latest, in case any changes are necessary following Kim's review of them.

Quarterly inquiry into turnover

IMPORTANT

Please read the notes before you fill in this form. Give the best estimates you can if you do not have exact figures.

FV			
T16/7704240000 72/112			

1. Details of business
Your business is classified as being in the industry described briefly in the letter accompanying this form. If you think this is wrong, please give a full description of your business. If you are involved in two or more activities, please describe the main one.

2. Period
Period for which you have filled in the form

		Day		Month		Year	
from		01	/	01	/	X4	11
to		31	/	03	/	X4	12

3. Turnover to the nearest £thousand (not including VAT)
Total turnover (including fees receivable)

184	40

4. Employees
Number of persons employed by the business at the end of the period covered by this return.

4.1	Total employees	13	50

of which

4.2	Full-time male	5	51
4.3	Part-time male	1	52
4.4	Full-time female	6	53
4.5	Part-time female	1	54

5. Other businesses included in this form
The form should be completed for the business named in the covering letter. If, exceptionally, you are unable to limit your return to the activities of this business, please list below the names and VAT registration numbers of the other businesses included.

Name of business
....

....

VAT registration number
....

....

(Please continue on a separate sheet if necessary)

REMARKS: If you have given any information which is significantly different from the last quarter, please explain.

PLEASE USE BLOCK CAPITALS

Name of person we should contact if necessary:		Kim Harvey		
Position in business:	Financial Controller		Date:	8/4/X4
Telephone no./ext:	020-7711 4240	Fax/Telex:	020-7711 4200	

Quarterly inquiry into capital expenditure

PLEASE COMPLETE AND RETURN THIS FORM BY 14 APRIL 20X4

FV	93	Q1
8100/7104420000		

IMPORTANT   Please read the enclosed notes before completing this form. If you do not have precise figures available give the best estimates you can. All values should be shown to the nearest £ thousand

1.   PERIOD (see note 1

			Day	Month	Year
Period covered by the return	from	08	01 /	01 /	X4
	to	09	31 /	03 /	X4

2.   LAND AND BUILDINGS (see note 2)   **£ thousand**

2.1 New building work or other constructional work of a capital nature (excluding the cost of land and of new dwellings)	10	24
2.2 Acquisition of land and of existing buildings	20	32
2.3 Proceeds of land and buildings disposed of	30	NIL

3.   VEHICLES (see note 3)

3.1 New and second-hand acquisitions	40	10
3.2 Proceeds of vehicles disposed of	50	5

4.   PLANT, MACHINERY etc (see note 4)

4.1 New and second-hand acquisitions	60	4
4.2 Proceeds of plant, machinery etc disposed of	70	3

5.   TOTAL

5.1 Total acquisitions (2.1 + 2.2 + 3.1 + 4.1)	90	70
5.2 Total disposals (2.3 + 3.2 + 4.2)	100	8

6.   FINANCE LEASING

6.1 Total amount included in acquisitions at 2.1, 3.1 and 4.1 for assets leased under finance leasing arrangements.	80	NIL

7.   COMMENTS ON UNUSUAL FLUCTUATIONS IN FIGURES WOULD BE APPRECIATED

....

Name of person to be contacted if necessary............KIM HARVEY....................................
BLOCK CAPITALS PLEASE

Position in company...FINANCIAL CONTROLLER   Signature.................................

Telephone No/Ext......020-7711 4240.........   Fax...020-7711 4200 Date...8 APRIL 20X4

Task 3

Quarter to	31 Mar 20X4		31 Dec 20X3		30 Sept 20X3		30 June 20X3	
College Division	£'000	%	£'000	%	£'000	%	£'000	%
Turnover	161.0	100.0	152.8	100.0	145.1	100.0	124.7	100.0
Direct costs	(70.8)	(44.0)	(68.4)	(44.8)	(66.7)	(46.0)	(64.1)	(51.4)
Other operating costs	(24.6)	(15.3)	(29.4)	(19.2)	(21.5)	(14.8)	(22.0)	(17.6)
Contribution	65.6	40.7	55.0	36.0	56.9	39.2	38.6	31.0
Bookshop								
Turnover	24.2	100.0	18.7	100.0	15.5	100.0	12.7	100.0
Cost of sales	(15.2)		(11.9)		(9.6)		(8.1)	
Gross profit	9.0	37.2	6.8	36.4	5.9	38.1	4.6	36.2
Staff costs	(4.4)		(4.3)		(4.1)		(4.2)	
Other operating costs	(2.8)		(2.2)		(2.0)		(2.4)	
Contribution	1.8	7.4	0.3	1.6	(0.2)	(1.3)	(2.0)	(15.7)
Bookshop staff nos.	1.5		1.5		1.5		1.0	
Sales per staff member (£'000)	16.1		12.5		10.3		12.7	

Task 4

(a)   *College Division*

Percentage of turnover

(b)   *Bookshop*

Quarter to	31 Mar 20X4	31 Dec 20X3	30 Sept 20X3	30 June 20X3

Sales per staff member (£'000)

| 20- |
| 15- |
| 10- |
| 5- | 16.1 | 12.5 | 10.3 | 12.7 |
| 0- |

Task 5

The measurement of the productivity of the teaching staff requires the establishment of an appropriate unit to measure the output of teachers.

If records are kept of the number of hours of contact between students and staff, productivity could be measured as lecture hours per teacher or student contact hours per teacher, where student contact hours equals the number of students in a lecture multiplied by the length of the lecture. Such measures might be applied to the teaching staff overall or to individual teachers.

If we want to measure the quality of teachers' work more closely, we might use records of the grades obtained by students and weight the output of teachers according to the grades of their students, thus awarding different teachers scores according to the performance of their students. This measure will require records on student grades to be maintained, and it may be seen as unfair if different student groups have different ability ranges.

BPP
PUBLISHING

ANSWER TO PRACTICE DEVOLVED ASSESSMENT 2: IRIS LTD

Task 1

Information from the sales report

Total sales, excluding VAT, are £1,044,980, and total VAT is £135,640.75.

The standard rated sales are £135,640.75/0.175 = £775,090.

The exempt sales are £(1,044,980 – 775,090) = £269,890.

Adjustments to the sales report figures

The sales of £16,000 invoiced in December but delivered in January must be added to the total of standard rated sales, because the tax point is December due to the early invoice. Similarly the sales of £24,600 delivered in September but invoiced in October must also be added since the tax point is October due to the issue of the invoice within 14 days after the basic tax point in September. The adjusted figures are as follows.

Total sales: £(1,044,980 + 16,000 + 24,600) = £1,085,580

Standard rated sales: £(775,090 + 16,000 + 24,600) = £815,690

Output VAT: £815,690 × 17.5% = £142,745.75

Exempt sales: £269,890

Recoverable percentage of unattributed input VAT: £815,690/£1,085,580 = 75.1%, rounded up to 76%.

Purchases

Total purchases are £644,953, and the total VAT is £72,563.40.

Bad debt relief

The total amount owed by the customer in liquidation, including VAT, was £7,600 × 1.175 = £8,930. Of this, £5,930 is still owing.

The bad debt, including VAT, is £5,930 × 60% = £3,558.

The VAT in this amount is £3,558 × 7/47 = £529.91.

Recoverable input VAT

	£
Attributable to taxable supplies £72,563.40 × 45%	32,653.53
Unattributable £72,563.40 × 35% (note 1) × 76%	19,301.86
	51,955.39
Bad debt relief	529.91
	52,485.30

Note 1: 100% total less 20% exempt less 45% standard rated = 35% non-attributable. Thus 35% of standard rated purchase were non-attributable.

The 'exempt input VAT' totals £20,608.01 (£72,563.40 – 32,653.53 – 19,301.86).

The '£625 a month on average' limit for exempt input VAT is clearly exceeded, so none of the exempt input VAT is recoverable.

The VAT return can now be completed.

Value Added Tax Return

For the period
01 10 X5 to 31 12 X5

For Official Use

Registration number

653 5306 77

Period

12 X5

You could be liable to a financial penalty if your completed return and all the VAT payable are not received by the due date.

Due date: 31 01 X6

IRIS LTD
1 FLOWER STREET
BLOOMTOWN
BL1 4LN

For Official Use

Your VAT Office telephone number is 0123-4567

ATTENTION

If this return and any tax due are not received by the due date you may be liable to a surcharge.

If you make supplies of goods to another EC Member State you are required to complete an EC Sales List (VAT 101).

Before you fill in this form please read the notes on the back and the VAT Leaflet *"Filling in your VAT return"*. Fill in all boxes clearly in ink, and write 'none' where necessary. Don't put a dash or leave any box blank. If there are no pence write "00" in the pence column. Do not enter more than one amount in any box.

For official use			£	p
	VAT due in this period on sales and other outputs	**1**	142,745	75
	VAT due in this period on acquisitions from other EC Member States	**2**	NONE	
	Total VAT due (the sum of boxes 1 and 2)	**3**	142,745	75
	VAT reclaimed in this period on purchases and other inputs (including acquisitions from the EC)	**4**	52,485	30
	Net VAT to be paid to Customs or reclaimed by you (Difference between boxes 3 and 4)	**5**	90,260	45
	Total value of sales and all other outputs excluding any VAT. Include your box 8 figure	**6**	1,085,580	00
	Total value of purchases and all other inputs excluding any VAT. Include your box 9 figure	**7**	644,953	00
	Total value of all supplies of goods and related services, excluding any VAT, to other EC Member States	**8**	NONE	00
	Total value of all acquisitions of goods and related services, excluding any VAT, from other EC Member States	**9**	NONE	00

If you are enclosing a payment please tick this box. ✓

DECLARATION: You, or someone on your behalf, must sign below.

I, *ANDREW TECH* .... declare that the
(Full name of signatory in BLOCK LETTERS)
information given above is true and complete.

Signature... *A Tech* .... Date *30/01* 20 *X6*

A false declaration can result in prosecution.

BPP
PUBLISHING

Task 2

DRAFT

Senior Accountant
Iris Ltd
1 Flower Street
Bloomtown
BL1 4LN

HM Customs & Excise
Excise House
Coventry

12.01.20X6

Dear Sir

CONFERENCE COSTS

We are due to hold a conference next month in Birmingham and the costs duly incurred will include approximately £3,000 of input VAT. I am writing to you for guidance with respect to the deductibility of the input VAT incurred.

The aim of the conference is to promote the name and products of Iris Ltd and delegates at the conference will comprise potential customers, current suppliers and our sales team.

I enclose a copy of the quotation received from the venue but in summary the costs incurred comprise room hire, equipment hire (to allow the showing of several promotional films) and lunchtime food and drink. The conference will run from 11am to 4pm.

If you require any further information or wish to discuss anything in more detail please do not hesitate to contact me. I look forward to your reply.

Your faithfully

Mr Jay

Senior Accountant

Task 3

MEMORANDUM

To: Finance Director
From: Accountant
Date: 29 January 20X6
Subject: Mistakes in VAT returns

Thank you for your memorandum dated 28 January.

(a)   If your friend makes errors on a VAT return, he can simply correct the error on a later return so long as the net error (error in output VAT net of error in input VAT) does not exceed £2,000. He should simply increase or reduce the figure in box 1, box 2 or box 4 as appropriate. If a figure becomes negative because of this, it should be shown in brackets.

       Errors exceeding £2,000 net must be separately notified to the local VAT office.

(b)   There are two penalties for understatements of the amount of VAT due. They are the misdeclaration penalty for very large errors and the misdeclaration penalty for repeated errors.

       The former penalty applies when the VAT which would have been lost equals or exceeds the lower of £1m or 30% of the sum of the correct input VAT and the correct output VAT.

       The latter penalty applies when there is a series of material inaccuracies, (ie errors) when the VAT which would have been lost equals or exceeds the lower of £500,000 or 10% of the sum of the correct input VAT and the correct output VAT. The first material inaccuracy leads to a penalty period of eight VAT return periods starting. Any material inaccuracies in that period, apart from the first one, incur the penalty.

       In both cases, the penalty is 15% of the VAT which would have been lost. If the penalty for very large errors applies to an error, the penalty for repeated errors cannot also apply but the error can lead to the start of a penalty period.

BPP
PUBLISHING

Task 4

> MEMORANDUM
>
> To: Data Processing Manager
> From: Accountant
> Date: 29 January 20X6
> Subject: New accounting software – rounding of VAT
>
> Thank you for your memorandum dated 28 January. The rules on the rounding of amounts of VAT are as follows.
>
> (a) If amounts of VAT are calculated for individual lines on an invoice, they must be:
>
> (i) rounded down to the nearest 0.1p, so 86.76p would be shown as 86.7p; or
>
> (ii) rounded to the nearest 0.5p, so 86.76p would be shown as 87p and 86.26p would be shown as 86.5p
>
> (b) If amounts of VAT are calculated from an amount of VAT per unit or article, the amount of VAT should be:
>
> (i) calculated to the nearest 0.01p and then rounded to the nearest 0.1p, so 0.24p would be rounded to 0.2p; or
>
> (ii) rounded to the nearest 0.5p, but with a minimum of 0.5p for any standard rated item, so 0.24p would be rounded to 0.5p rather than to 0p.
>
> (c) The total VAT shown on an invoice should be rounded down to the nearest 1p, so £32.439 would be shown as £32.43.

Answers to trial run devolved assessment

ANSWERS TO TRIAL RUN DEVOLVED ASSESSMENT: MYLLTON LTD

Task 1

2001	Monthly purchases at invoiced prices, including VAT £'000	Index of materials purchased by the Wood and Wood Products Industry, 1996 = 100	Value of timber purchases at current prices, including VAT £'000
January	138	96.9	134
February	173	96.2	166
March	147	95.8	141
April	171	95.8	164
May	138	95.7	132
June	232	95.5	222
July	209	95.2	199
August	196	95.0	186
September	274	94.6	259
October	225	94.3	212
November	201	94.4	190
December	183	94.4	173
Total	2,287	na	2,178

Note. The precise total for the adjusted purchases, to the nearest £'000, is £2,177,000. The difference between this and the figure shown is caused by rounding the figures for each month in column three to the nearest £'000 before calculating the total. However, £2,178,000 is the figure required as it is obtained by complying with the instructions.

BPP PUBLISHING

Task 2

	£'000
Value of timber purchases at current prices, including VAT	2,178
VAT included above at 17.5%	324
Value of timber purchases at current prices, excluding VAT	1,854

Task 3

MEMO

To: Romy Gurlane

From: Olivia Tran

Subject: Effect of Graviner Ltd's use of 1996 transfer prices for timber during 2001

Date: 2 August 2002

The table below sets out the comparative figures for 2001 that you requested.

	Using 2001 accounts	*Using current indexed values for timber purchased from Graviner Ltd*
Gross profit percentage	23%	26%
Net profit percentage	6%	8%
Return on capital employed (ROCE)	12%	16%

★ ROCE = Net profit ÷ capital employed

Workings for Task 3

	Figures contained in 2001 accounts	*Figures using indexed value for timber purchased from Graviner*
	£'000	*£'000*
Sales	**4,264**	**4,264**
Timber purchases from Graviner	1,946	1,854
Other material purchases	328	328
Production labour	739	739
Production overheads	254	254
Gross profit	**997**	**1,089**
Administration overheads	476	476
Selling and distribution costs	198	198
Other non-production costs	57	57
Net profit	266	358
Fixed assets (net book value)	1,847	1,847
Current assets	638	638
Current liabilities	204	204
Capital employed	2,281	2,281

Task 4

Timber and Ancillary Trades Federation

Gloster House, 33 Loville Road, Dartford, Kent DA8 3QQ

TURNOVER AND COSTS RETURN 2001

Company or Business Name	Hexa-Gann Group Plc
Membership number	H920/58
Accounting year end date	31 December 2001
Period covered by figures, if less than one year	na
	£m
Turnover	15,738
Timber purchases	7,938
Production labour costs	1,999
Other production costs	1,177
Non-production costs	1,838
Total costs	12,952

Notes.
1. All figures should exclude VAT.
2. All figures should be to the nearest £100,000 and expressed as decimal millions (eg £31,832,420 would be £31.8)
3. This return should be signed by an officer of the company, or the owner or a partner if unincorporated.

Signature:

Name:

Position:

Date:

Please return to Annabelle Peruke at the above address by 6 August 2002, marked 'Private & Confidential'.

Workings for Task 4

	Graviner Ltd £'000	Myllton Ltd £'000	Total £'000
Sales (including sales to other members of the Hexa-Gann Group)	13,420	4,264	
Less sales to Myllton Ltd		1,946	
Net sales	**13,420**	**2,318**	**15,738**
Timber purchases (all from outside the Hexa-Gann Group)	**7,938**		**7,938**
Production labour costs	**1,260**	**739**	**1,999**
Other material purchases	276	328	
Production overheads	319	254	
Other production costs	**595**	**582**	**1,177**
Administration overheads	684	476	
Selling and distribution costs	276	198	
Other non-production costs	147	57	
Non-production costs	**1107**	**731**	**1,838**
Total costs	**10,900**	**2,052**	**12,952**

Task 5

MEMO

To: Nigel Lyte

From: Olivia Tran

Subject: TATF Turnover and Costs Return 2001

Date: 2 August 2002

I enclose the above return , duly completed, for your authorisation prior to despatch.

Please note that the due date for its return to the TATF is Monday 6 August. May I please have your authorisation to send it by Special Delivery.

Task 6

MYLLTON LTD

PRODUCTIVITY REPORT

Period	Standard Hours produced (3 month total)	Production labour hours wor`ked (3 month total)	Output hours per input hour
March 02 to May 02	20,280	21,311	0.952
April 02 to June 02	19,915	20,715	0.961
May 02 to July 02	21,340	21,630	0.987

Task 7

Value Added Tax Return
For the period
01 05 02 to 31 07 02

For Official Use

Registration number | Period

578 4060 20 | 07 02

You could be liable to a financial penalty if your completed return and all the VAT payable are not received by the due date.

Due date: 31 08 02

081 578 4060 19 100 03 98   Q35192

James Mbanu
Myllton Ltd
23 Cavour Road
Bridge Trading Estate
New Sarum SP0 7YT   219921/10

For Official Use

ATTENTION

Your VAT Office telephone number is 01682-386000

If this return and any tax due are not received by the due date you may be liable to a surcharge.

If you make supplies of goods to another EC Member State you are required to complete an EC Sales List (VAT 101).

Before you fill in this form please read the notes on the back and the VAT Leaflet *"Filling in your VAT return"*.
Fill in all boxes clearly in ink, and write 'none' where necessary. Don't put a dash or leave any box blank. If there are no pence write "00" in the pence column. Do not enter more than one amount in any box.

For official use			£	p
	VAT due in this period on sales and other outputs	**1**	186,607	34
	VAT due in this period on acquisitions from other EC Member States	**2**	2,291	54
	Total VAT due (the sum of boxes 1 and 2)	**3**	188,898	88
	VAT reclaimed in this period on purchases and other inputs (including acquisitions from the EC)	**4**	103,524	83
	Net VAT to be paid to Customs or reclaimed by you (Difference between boxes 3 and 4)	**5**	85,374	05
	Total value of sales and all other outputs excluding any VAT. Include your box 8 figure	**6**	1,066,327	00
	Total value of purchases and all other inputs excluding any VAT. Include your box 9 figure	**7**	716,250	00
	Total value of all supplies of goods and related services, excluding any VAT, to other EC Member States	**8**	Nil	00
	Total value of all acquisitions of goods and related services, excluding any VAT, from other EC Member States	**9**	13,094	00

If you are enclosing a payment please tick this box. ☑

DECLARATION: You, or someone on your behalf, must sign below.

I, ...**James Mbanu**.. declare that the
(Full name of signatory in BLOCK LETTERS)
information given above is true and complete.

Signature.. Date **2 Aug** 20 **02**

A false declaration can result in prosecution.

F

0196929   IB (October 2000)

VAT 100 (Half)

Calculations for Box 4

	£
VAT on purchases from UK suppliers	105,473.43
less VAT on car purchased (not exclusively for business use)	(4,978.90)
plus VAT on acquisions from EC member states (Box 2)	2,291.54
plus VAT bad debt relief being claimed	738.76
	103,524.83

Task 8

MYLLTON LTD

23 Cavour Road, Bridge Trading Estate, New Sarum SPO 7YT
Telephone 01722-883567

HM Customs & Excise
Roebuck House
24-28 Bedford Place
Southampton SO15 2DB

2 August 2002

Dear Sirs,

Registration number: 578 4060 20

The company is proposing to host a canal boat evening during August 2002 for its staff and representatives of its customers. An evening meal will be provided, together with music and a free bar. This is a standard package supplied by Knet Cruises Ltd, who are registered for VAT.

As VAT can only be reclaimed in respect of staff entertainment we are not clear as to how the VAT element of the supplier's invoice should be treated.

I would welcome your advice as to the correct treatment for VAT purposes of this supply.

Yours faithfully

Olivia Tran
Deputy Accountant

Registered office: 23 Cavour Road, Bridge Trading Estate, New Sarum SPO 7YT
Registered in England, number 2314562

144

Answers to AAT Sample simulation

ANSWERS TO AAT SAMPLE SIMULATION: HODDLE LTD

Task 1

Engineering Supplies Limited invoice

This is a valid VAT-only invoice. It should be processed as a March input and the VAT should be reclaimed in the quarter January to March 2002.

Alpha Stationery invoice

This is a valid VAT invoice of the less detailed kind. It should be processed as a March input and the VAT should be reclaimed in the quarter January to March 2002.

Jamieson & Co invoice

This is merely a proforma invoice. The service provided by Jamieson & Co cannot be regarded as an input until a valid invoice is received. The VAT should not be reclaimed at this stage.

Task 2

Value Added Tax Return
For the period
01 01 02 **to** 31 03 02

For Official Use

Registration number	Period
578 4060 19	03 02

You could be liable to a financial penalty if your completed return and all the VAT payable are not received by the due date.

Due date: 31 04 02

081 578 4060 19 100 03 98   Q35192
MR SHERRY TEDDINGHAM
HODDLE LIMITED
22 FORMGUARD STREET
PEXLEY
PY6 3QW
219921/10

For Official Use

ATTENTION

If this return and any tax due are not received by the due date you may be liable to a surcharge.

If you make supplies of goods to another EC Member State you are required to complete an EC Sales List (VAT 101).

Your VAT Office telephone number is 01682 386000

Before you fill in this form please read the notes on the back and the VAT Leaflet *"Filling in your VAT return"*.
Fill in all boxes clearly in ink, and write 'none' where necessary. Don't put a dash or leave any box blank. If there are no pence write "00" in the pence column. Do not enter more than one amount in any box.

For official use			£	p
	VAT due in this period on sales and other outputs	**1**	7,740	12
	VAT due in this period on acquisitions from other EU Member States	**2**	NONE	
	Total VAT due (the sum of boxes 1 and 2)	**3**	7,740	12
	VAT reclaimed in this period on purchases and other inputs (including acquisitions from the EU)	**4**	13,477	96
	Net VAT to be paid to Customs or reclaimed by you (Difference between boxes 3 and 4)	**5**	(5,737	84)
	Total value of sales and all other outputs excluding any VAT. Include your box 8 figure	**6**	120,606	00
	Total value of purchases and all other inputs excluding any VAT. Include your box 9 figure	**7**	80,727	00
	Total value of all supplies of goods and related services, excluding any VAT, to other EU Member States	**8**	10,870	00
	Total value of all acquisitions of goods and related services, excluding any VAT, from other EU Member States	**9**	NONE	00

If you are enclosing a payment please tick this box.	DECLARATION: You, or someone on your behalf, must sign below.
✓	I, *SHERRY TEDDINGHAM* .... declare that the (Full name of signatory in BLOCK LETTERS) information given above is true and complete. Signature.. Date *9 April* 20 02 **A false declaration can result in prosecution.**

F

0196929   IB (October 2000)

VAT 100 (Half)

★See page 154 for workings

Task 3

HODDLE LIMITED

22 Formguard Street, Pexley PY6 3QW
Telephone 01682 431 432256

9 April 2002

HM Customs & Excise
Brendon House
14 Abbey Street
Pexley PY2 3WR

Dear Sirs

Registration number: 578 4060 19

The company at present accounts for VAT on the basis of invoices raised and received. We are considering the idea of changing to the cash accounting scheme, and I would be grateful if you could provide some information on this. Perhaps there is a leaflet setting out details of the scheme?

The particular points of which we are uncertain are as follows.

- What turnover limits apply to the scheme? Are these limits affected by the fact that this company is part of a group consisting of the company itself and its parent company?

- How are bad debts accounted for under the cash accounting scheme?

I would be grateful for any assistance you are able to give on these points and generally about the workings of the scheme.

Yours faithfully

Sherry Teddingham

ACCOUNTANT

Registered office: 22 Formguard Street, Pexley PY6 3QW
Registered in England, number 2314561

Task 4

CONSOLIDATED PROFIT AND LOSS ACCOUNT
FOR THE THREE MONTHS ENDED 31 MARCH 2002

	Kelly £	Hoddle £	Adjustments £	Consolidated £
Sales	295,768	120,607	20,167	396,208
Opening stock	28,341	14,638		42,979
Purchases	136,095	50,908	18,271	168,732
	164,436	65,546		211,711
Closing stock	31,207	16,052	1,896	49,155
Cost of sales	133,229	*49,494		162,556
Gross profit	162,539	71,113		233,652
Wages and salaries	47,918	18,014		65,932
Distribution expenses	28,341	13,212		41,553
Administration expenses	30,189	11,676		41,865
Stationery	2,541	*544		3,085
Travel	2,001	267		2,268
Office expenses	3,908	737		4,645
Interest payable	12,017			12,017
Other expenses	11,765	3,384		15,149
	138,680	47,834		186,514
Net profit for the period	23,859	23,279		47,138

* See page 154 for workings.

Task 4

Helping hand. You did not have to fill in the figures on this schedule but you would probably have found it helpful to do so.

QUARTERLY CONSOLIDATED PROFIT AND LOSS ACCOUNTS FOR THE YEAR ENDED 31 MARCH 2002

	1 April 2001-30 June 2001 £	1 July 2001-30 September 2001 £	1 October 2001-31 December 2001 £	1 January 2002-31 March 2002 £	1 April 2001-31 March 2002 £
Sales	325,719	275,230	306,321	396,208	1,303,478
Cost of sales	134,861	109,421	121,358	162,556	528,196
Gross profit	190,858	165,809	184,963	233,652	775,282
Wages and salaries	63,314	61,167	64,412	65,932	254,825
Distribution expenses	34,217	30,135	31,221	41,553	137,126
Administration expenses	34,765	33,012	36,415	41,865	146,057
Stationery	2,981	2,671	3,008	3,085	11,745
Travel	1,975	1,876	2,413	2,268	8,532
Office expenses	4,412	4,713	3,083	4,645	16,853
Interest payable	12,913	12,714	12,432	12,017	50,076
Other expenses	10,981	16,421	15,431	15,149	57,982
	165,558	162,709	168,415	186,514	683,196
Net profit for the period	25,300	3,100	16,548	47,138	92,086

151

BPP PUBLISHING

Task 5

REPORT

To: Sherry Teddingham
From: Sol Bellcamp
Subject: Report on group results for the year ended 31 March 2002
Date: 9 April 2002

Introduction

This report contains the usual information on group results for the year, plus the additional information requested in your memo to me of 2 April 2002.

Key ratios

Gross profit margin = £775,282 ÷ £1,303,478 = 59.5%
Net profit margin = £92,086 ÷ £1,303,478 = 7.1%
Return on shareholders' capital employed = £92,086 ÷ £1,034,708 = 8.9%

Sales revenue by quarter

Quarter	Indexed £	Indexed (base period = first quarter 2000/01) £
Apr - June 2001	325,719	315,511
Jul - Sep 2001	275,230	264,175
Oct - Dec 2001	306,321	291,005
Jan - Mar 2002	396,208	379,822

Pie chart showing sales by quarter

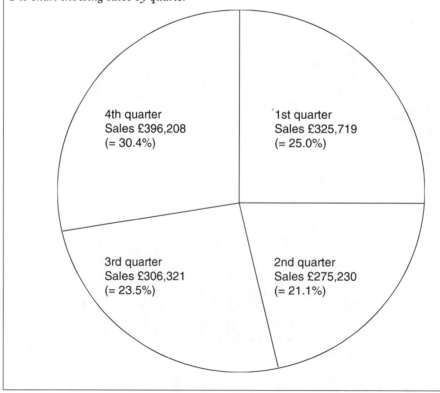

Task 6

INTERFIRM COMPARISON DATA (extracts)

Name of company............Kelly Limited and subsidiary..............................

Year ended ....31 March 2002..................................

Data

	£	% of sales	Industry best	Industry average
Sales	1,303,478			
Gross profit	775,282	59.5%	62.1%	57.3%
Net profit	92,086	7.1%	10.4%	5.8%
Fixed assets	1,229,348			
Current assets	325,703			
Current liabilities	148,271			
Return on capital employed		10.1%	10.3%	9.0%

Task 7

MEMO

To: Sherry Teddingham

From: Sol Bellcamp

Subject: Interfirm comparison data

Date: 9 April 2002

I enclose the completed interfirm comparison data for the year ended 31 March 2002. Please let me know if you disagree with anything in it; otherwise, it is ready for despatch subject to your authorisation.

Workings

Task 2

		£
Box 4	PDB	12,690.53
	Petty cash	244.95
	Bad debt	73.50
	Engineering Supplies invoice	466.77
	Alpha Stationery invoice	2.21
		13,477.96
Box 7	PDB	79,179.67
	Petty cash	1,535.34
	Alpha Stationery invoice	12.63
		80,727.64

Task 4

Hoddle's cost of sales, January - March 2002

	£
Opening stock	14,638.00
Purchases	50,908.21
	65,546.21
Closing stock	16,052.00
Cost of sales	49,494.21

Hoddle's stationery costs, January - March 2002

	£
Petty cash book	531.55
Alpha Stationery invoice	12.63
	544.18

Lecturers' resource pack activities

CHAPTER 1: THE ORGANISATION, ACCOUNTING AND REPORTING

1   FACTORS   **Pre-assessment**

What three factors have an effect on an organisation's accounting system?

2   GEOGRAPHY   **Pre-assessment**

How are the accounting procedures of an organisation specifically affected by geography?

BPP PUBLISHING

CHAPTER 2: BUSINESS AND ACCOUNTING INFORMATION

3   **CORPORATE REPORT**   **Pre-assessment**

The Corporate Report is a publication which argued that companies do not provide enough information about themselves. What are the desirable qualities of accounting reports as listed by *The Corporate Report*?

CHAPTER 3: STATISTICAL INFORMATION

4 SECONDARY DATA

Secondary data is:

A   Data that does not provide any information
B   Data collected for another purpose
C   Data collected specifically for the purpose of the survey being undertaken
D   Data collected by post or telephone, not by personal interview

5 BLANKS

Fill in the blanks in the statements below using the words in the box.

Data can be either (1) .... (have variables) or (2) ....
(have (3) ....). Variables can be either (4) .... (eg 0, 1,
2, 3) or (5) .... (eg 0.54, 0.612, 0.117). Data may also be classified as
(6) .... (collected for a specific survey) or (7) ....
(collected for some other purpose).

• Quantitative	• Continuous	• Attributes	• Primary
• Secondary	• Qualitative	• Discrete	

CHAPTER 4: PRESENTING INFORMATION: GRAPHS

6   OGIVE   Assessment

A grouped frequency distribution for the volume of output produced at a factory over a period of 40 weeks is as follows.

Output (units)	Number of times output achieved
> 0 ≤ 200	4
>200 ≤ 400	8
>400 ≤ 600	12
>600 ≤ 800	10
>800 ≤ 1,000	6
	40

Task

Draw an appropriate ogive, and estimate the number of weeks in which output was 550 units or less.

7   AXES   Assessment

A graph has a **horizontal axis**, the x axis, and a **vertical axis**, the y axis.

- The x axis is used to represent the .... variable.

- The y axis is used to represent the .... variable.

CHAPTER 5: PRESENTING INFORMATION: TABLES AND CHARTS

8   CHAWLEY PLASTICS LTD   Assessment

The management of Chawley Plastics Ltd wish to present some information about results to employees. It has been decided that a visual form of display would be the best way to communicate the information.

The relevant data are as follows.

	20X8 £'000	20X7 £'000	20X6 £'000	20X5 £'000	20X4 £'000
Sales	5.2	5.1	4.8	4.0	3.5
Costs					
Direct materials	1.5	1.4	1.2	1.0	0.8
Direct wages	2.3	1.8	1.6	1.3	1.0
Production overhead	0.7	0.7	0.6	0.5	0.4
Other overhead	0.6	0.5	0.4	0.3	0.2
Taxation	0.0	0.3	0.4	0.3	0.3
Profit	0.1	0.4	0.6	0.6	0.8

Product groups, as a percentage of total sales

Product group	20X8 %	20X7 %	20X6 %	20X5 %	20X4 %
W	33	36	38	30	25
X	5	10	12	18	25
Y	46	36	30	30	25
Z	16	18	20	22	25
	100	100	100	100	100

Tasks

Prepare two different visual displays to show:

(a) Sales by product group.

(b) A comparison of 20X7 with 20X8, analysing total sales into costs, taxation and profit, with particular emphasis on direct wages.

9   AGRICULTURAL PRODUCTS   Assessment

The management of a company which relies heavily on the export of agricultural products has included the following paragraph in a report.

Percentage shares of output in the industrialised countries

We can appreciate the changes in the percentage shares of output in the industrialised countries represented by agriculture, services and industry by taking three years - 1970, 1984 and 1999 - as examples. The percentage share of agriculture declined from 7.2% in 1970 to 4.9% by 1984. The share of agriculture had fallen to 2.9% by 1999. The share of industry also declined over this period, falling to 32.7% in 1999 compared with 37.3% in 1984 and 40.2% in 1970. The remaining share is that of services, which had swelled to 64.4% of output by 1999 compared with 52.6% in 1970.

Task

Show the above information in the form of pie charts.

CHAPTER 6: AVERAGES AND TIME SERIES

10   QUARTERLY PROFITS   **Assessment**

The following is a time series of an organisation's quarterly profits.

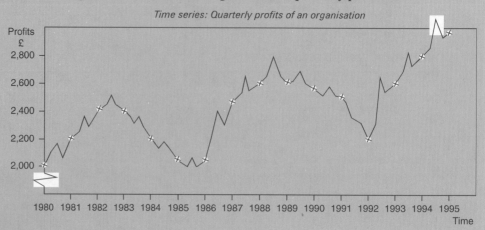

Time series: Quarterly profits of an organisation

Task

Explain, and comment on the limitations of:

(a)   The long-term trend
(b)   The cyclical movement
(c)   Seasonal variations

11   MOVING AVERAGES   **Assessment**

Using the following data, what is the **three-month moving average** for April?

	Number of new houses
Month	*finished*
January	500
February	450
March	700
April	900
May	1,250
June	1,000

CHAPTER 7: USING INDEX NUMBERS

| 12 | **UK RETAIL CHAINS** | **Assessment** |

A company is engaged in the business of assembling toys and consumer durables which it then sells direct to major UK retail chains. Management wishes to present a series of data showing sales in real terms over recent years.

Task

Giving reasons, explain which of the following indices would be most appropriate for adjusting the monetary sales figures of the company into 'real' terms.

(a)   General index of retail prices (RPI)
(b)   Producer prices index: materials and fuels
(c)   Producer prices: manufactured goods

| 13 | **REPORTING AGENCY** | **Assessment** |

The Reporting Agency (a fictitious government agency) was set a target for 20X6/X7 of reducing the unit cost of producing a report by 3.5% in real terms. In accordance with Treasury guidelines, the GDP deflator is to be used to adjust from cash terms to real terms.

The average cost of producing a report in cash terms was £37.24 in 20X6/X7, compared with £37.64 in 20X5/X6, again in cash terms.

Figures for the GDP deflator are as follows.

20X4/X5	100.0
20X5/X6	103.7
20X6/X7	106.9

Task

Prepare a table for inclusion in a management report showing whether or not the Agency met its target.

| 14 | **CLOVERDALE LTD** | **Assessment** |

Sales growth for Cloverdale Ltd over the past five years has been as follows.

Turnover	£m
20X2	33.7
20X3	37.2
20X4	40.1
20X5	42.3
20X6	44.1

The Retail Prices Index for these years was as follows.

20X2	139.2
20X3	141.9
20X4	146.0
20X5	150.7
20X6	155.1

Task

Convert the figures to real terms based on 20X6, and show the real annual year-on-year growth in turnover.

CHAPTER 8: WRITING REPORTS AND COMPLETING FORMS

15   COMPLETING FORMS   **Assessment**

The following table shows details of Penny Farthing Ltd's employees from 1 December 20X6 to 30 June 20X7.

Summary of employees who were employed by Penny Farthing Ltd during the six months to 30 June 20X7

Employee's initials	Age	Male/female	Full/part time	Date of joining/leaving
ARB	27	M	F	Joined 18.11.X5
NC	34	F	F	Joined 1.11.X6
ROD	37	M	P	Joined 1.3.X2; left 31.5.X7
RJ	47	M	P	Joined 20.1.X7
ALK	26	F	F	Joined 1.10.X6
PRM	38	M	P	Joined 24.8.X1
IP	34	M	P	Joined 29.9.X4
JJS	49	M	P	Joined 12.4.X3
RT	41	M	F	Joined 12.8.X6
FWT	36	M	F	Joined 2.1.X7
SRW	29	F	F	Joined 5.3.X7
TW	35	F	F	Joined 15.5.X5; left 20.3.X7
VAW	27	F	P	Joined 1.4.X6; left 15.4.X7

Complete Sections 2 and 4 of the following form from the Office for National Statistics.

A compulsory inquiry conducted by
the Government Statistical Service
IN CONFIDENCE

Office for National Statistics

Office for National Statistics
Newport, Gwent NP9 1XG

Penny Farthing Ltd
14 Church Street
Swindon
Wiltshire
SN21 7QZ

Our ref TI5/404140000 96/941
Please give this reference number if you contact us

Please correct any errors in name, address or postcode
Inquiries into turnover of transport businesses

SECOND QUARTER 20X7 (1 APRIL 20X7 TO 30 JUNE 20X7)

Notice under Section 1 of the Statistics of Trade Act 1947

Dear Contributor

Every quarter we send out this inquiry to obtain up-to-date statistics about transport businesses. All larger businesses and a sample of smaller ones are included. Your business has been included in the inquiry.

Your figures will be used with those from other businesses to provide government with information about developments in your sector and in the economy. Together with other information, this is an essential part of economic forecasting and policy making.

The inquiry results contribute to quarterly estimates of Gross Domestic Product which are published in an ONS press notice and in other ONS publications.

Because of the importance of the information, this is a statutory inquiry. *Under the Act of 1947, it is compulsory for you to provide the information. This should be returned within three weeks of the end of the period which it covers.* The information you provide will be treated as strictly confidential as required by the Act. I can assure you that it will not be revealed in published statistics in a way which would allow anybody to identify your business or be given to any unauthorised person without your permission.

To save you time, we have made the form as short as possible. There are notes to help you but if you have any difficulties or need more information, my staff on the telephone number shown above will be pleased to assist. If exact figures are not available, informed estimates will do. If you need additional copies of the form, please let us know.

Please accept my thanks for your co-operation. Without this we could not provide a good service to government.

Yours sincerely,

Official use only	
Rec only	
Receipted	
Data pre T/O	
On line TO	
P/A	

Business Statistics Division

IMPORTANT

FV				
T15/4 0414000096/941				

Please read the notes before you fill in this form. Give the best estimates you can if you do not have exact figures.

1. **Details of business**
   Your business is classified as being in the industry described briefly in the letter accompanying this form. If you think this is wrong, please give a full description of your business. If you are involved in two or more activities, please describe the main one.

2. **Period**
   Period for which you have filled in the form

	Day	Month	Year	
from	/	/		11
to	/	/		12

3. **Turnover** to the nearest £thousand (not including VAT)
   Total turnover (including fees receivable)

	40

4. **Employees**
   Number of persons employed by the business at the end of the period covered by this return.

4.1 Total employees		50

   of which

4.2 Full-time male		51
4.3 Part-time male		52
4.4 Full-time female		53
4.5 Part-time female		54

5. **Other businesses included in this form**
   The form should be completed for the business named in the covering letter. If, exceptionally, you are unable to limit your return to the activities of this business, please list below the names and VAT registration numbers of the other businesses included.

   Name of business   VAT registration number
   ....
   ....

   (Please continue on a separate sheet if necessary)

   REMARKS: If you have given any information which is significantly different from the last quarter, please explain.
   ....
   ....
   ......

   PLEASE USE BLOCK CAPITALS
   Name of person we should contact if necessary:
   Position in business: Date:
   Telephone no./ext: Fax/Telex:

NOTES ON FILLING IN THIS FORM

Quarterly inquiries into turnover

Period

Your return should cover the three months shown on the front of the form. If you do not have figures for that period, the return may be made for the nearest period of a similar length as long as it relates mainly to the one specified. It is important that there are no gaps or overlaps with this period and the period covered by any previous returns that you have made to this inquiry.

Turnover

Give the total amount receivable by the business for services provided or goods sold during the period covered by the form. These amounts should not include VAT. Do not include any amounts receivable from selling or transferring capital assets. The figure given should be for services or goods which you have invoiced rather than cash which you have received, unless a figure for invoiced amounts is not readily available. It is important that the figure is given on a consistent basis from quarter to quarter. Show it to the nearest £ thousand. For example £27,025 should be shown as 27.

Scope of the inquiry

Your turnover should include any business activities carried out within the United Kingdom, (that is England, Scotland, Wales and Northern Ireland). This should include work done in connection with overseas contracts or activities for which invoices are issued by you in the United Kingdom.

Employees

Include full-time and part-time employees (part-time means those who normally work 30 hours a week or less); temporary and casual workers; those off sick, on holiday or on short-term; youth training scheme trainees who have a contract of employment and employment trainees on continuation training; employees who work away from the workplace such as sales reps and lorry drivers.

Exclude those employed by outside contractors or agencies, working proprietors, partners, self-employed, directors not on contract; youth training scheme or employment training trainees without a contract of employment; home workers on piecework rates; former employees still on payroll as pensioners; those who normally work at another establishment such as temporary transfers and secondments.

CHAPTER 9: REPORTING PERFORMANCE

16   BB LIMITED   **Assessment**

BB LIMITED
DEPARTMENTAL TRADING AND PROFIT AND LOSS ACCOUNTS
FOR THE YEAR ENDED 30 SEPTEMBER 20X1

	Dept X		*Dept Y*	
	£	£	£	£
Sales		90,000		135,000 [1]
Cost of sales:				
Opening stock	18,000		22,500	
Purchases	52,500 [2]		81,000	
	70,500		103,500	
Less closing stock	19,500		27,000	
		51,000		76,500
Gross profit		39,000		58,500
Less expenses:				
Selling & distribution	11,400		17,100	
Administration	8,725		13,225	
Lighting & heating	500		2,400	
Rent & rates	9,500		4,750	
		30,125		37,475
Net profit		8,875		21,025

Note

(1) Includes sales to the furniture department at cost of £11,500.

(2) This figure includes purchases from the electrical goods department of £11,500.

Task

Calculate the consolidated trading and profit and loss account for BB Limited for the year ended 30 September 20X1 showing clearly any adjustments which should be made.

CHAPTER 10: MEASURING PERFORMANCE

The following data is required for Lecturers' practice activities 17-20.

RAYTONBANK FOODS LTD
FINANCIAL RESULTS FOR THE SIX MONTHS TO JUNE 20X7

Store	Whitby	Scarboro	Stokesley	Guisboro	York	Thirsk	Malton	Total
Total sales area (sq ft)	11,000	12,500	9,700	9,500	13,500	9,800	8,750	74,750
Full-time equivalent employees (June)	55	60	45	45	60	40	40	345
	£'000	£'000	£'000	£'000	£'000	£'000	£'000	£'000
Turnover	3,871	4,309	3,212	3,188	4,253	2,817	2,400	24,050
Operating expenses	3,633	4,051	3,022	2,999	3,989	2,650	2,270	22,614
Net profit	238	258	190	189	264	167	130	1,436
Operating expenses include:								
Wages and salaries	341	380	272	271	379	250	250	2,143
Depreciation	25	28	22	22	31	23	19	170
Bought out items, goods and services	3,267	3,643	2,728	2,706	3,579	2,377	2,001	20,301

The weekly sales figures for the six months to June 20X7 are as follows.

(*Note*. The weekly periods for which sales statistics are collected do not correspond with the ends of months. For accounting purposes, the company treats the end of the month as falling on the Saturday closest to the end of the calendar month.)

Accounting month ending Saturday	Sales £	Number of weeks
1 February	4,625,810	5
1 March	3,808,701	4
29 March	3,698,125	4
3 May	4,494,205	5
31 May	3,774,887	4
28 June 20X7	3,648,221	4

An analysis of the company's employees at the beginning and end of the six months to June 20X7 shows the following.

	Number employed		Full-time equivalent	
	29.12.X6	28.6.X7	29.12.X6	28.6.X7
Full-time male	116	110	116	110
Full-time female	188	190	188	190
Part-time male	27	25	13	12
Part-time female	71	75	31	33
	402	400	348	345

17   KEY PERFORMANCE RATIOS   Assessment

Prepare the following key performance ratios and other statistics for Raytonbank Foods Ltd for the six month period to June 20X7, for each store and for the business as a whole.

1   Turnover per employee
2   Net profit per employee
3   Sales per square foot
4   Wages and salaries per employee
5   Value added per employee
6   Value added per £1 of employee costs
7   % net profit to sales

BPP PUBLISHING

NB. Value added is defined as Turnover *less* Bought out items, goods and services.

Employee costs comprise wages and salaries.

In calculating these ratios, use full-time equivalents for employee numbers.

18 GROCERY   Assessment

The following UK average grocery retail productivity measures are available. 'Employee' for these purposes means 'full-time equivalent employee'.

	£
Annual turnover per employee	140,842
Annual net profit per employee	8,752
Annual wages/salaries per employee	13,941
Weekly sales per sq ft of sales area	17.00

Prepare a table comparing the above productivity measures for Raytonbank Foods Ltd for the six months to June 20X7 with the UK average productivity measures.

19 RAYTONBANK FOODS   Assessment

The relationship of net profit to turnover as a percentage in this type of business is typically low. Grocery retail businesses generally combine high sales volume with a low profit margin.

Using the figures for Raytonbank Foods Ltd for the six months to June 20X7, present a component bar chart to show how overall turnover is related to the different categories of operating expenses and net profit.

20 JULY   Assessment

Starting on Sunday 29 June 20X7, the stores in Stokesley, Guisborough, Thirsk and Malton began opening on Sundays as part of an experiment.

Sales figures for the stores in the 4-week accounting month of July 20X7 are as follows.

		Wh	*Sc*	*St*	*Gu*	*Yo*	*Th*	*Ma*
Week ending		£'000	£'000	£'000	£'000	£'000	£'000	£'000
5 July	Sun	-	-	20	24	-	17	15
	Mon - Sat	147	167	120	117	166	93	80
12 July	Sun	-	-	19	22	-	14	20
	Mon - Sat	158	159	122	120	172	94	84
19 July	Sun	-	-	16	19	-	14	20
	Mon - Sat	159	182	127	123	176	99	87
26 July	Sun	-	-	14	18	-	13	14
	Mon - Sat	161	177	126	122	175	96	76

Prepare a *table* showing the percentage change in average weekly turnover for each store for July compared with each store's average weekly turnover in the half year before the start of Sunday opening. In the table, group together:

(a) Those stores which have begun Sunday opening, and
(b) Those which have not.

CHAPTERS 11 AND 12: PREPARING VAT RETURNS

The following information relates to Practice activities 21-30.

The following documents relate to Strode Ltd for the three months ended 30 June 20X3. All transactions were with persons in the United Kingdom.

SUMMARY OF SUPPLIES MADE			
(Some columns not shown)			
Date	*Item*	*VAT rate*	*Net amount*
		%	£
2.4.X3	Stockbroking services	Exempt	62,000
12.4.X3	Sale of books about finance	0.0	27,000
21.4.X3	Stockbroking services	Exempt	35,250
30.4.X3	Stockbroking services	Exempt	24,870
2.5.X3	Sale of books about finance	0.0	33,500
12.5.X3	Investment advice	17.5	3,850
28.5.X3	Trust administration services	17.5	11,250
4.6.X3	Sale of books	0.0	7,500
10.6.X3	Investment advice	17.5	8,500
17.6.X3	Insurance broking services for a UK company	Exempt	1,800
30.6.X3	Stockbroking services	Exempt	32,000

SUMMARY OF SUPPLIES RECEIVED			
(Some columns not shown)			
Date	*Item*	*VAT rate*	*Net amount*
		%	£
1.4.X3	New car for managing director	17.5	15,000
12.4.X3	Petrol	17.5	600
2.5.X3	Office furniture	17.5	5,400
3.6.X3	Stationery	17.5	7,400
15.6.X3	Computer bureau services	17.5	22,000
17.6.X3	Staff Summer Ball	17.5	13,617

MEMORANDUM

To: Accountant
From: Finance director
Date: 10 July 20X3
Subject: Your memo of 6 July 20X3

Thank you for your enquiries. I can reply as follows.

(a) The managing director was supplied with fuel free of charge for both business and private use. The car has a 1,800 cc petrol engine. The scale charge per quarter is £286.

(b) I agree that in the tax period ended 31 March 20X3 the company's output VAT was understated by £870.

MEMORANDUM

To: Accountant
From: Personnel department
Date: 7 July 20X3
Subject: Staff Summer Ball

The staff summer ball cost:

	£
Hire of venue and staff	5,000
Catering - food	5,000
- drinks	5,000
Band	1,000
	16,000

The above figures are inclusive of VAT where applicable.

The total cost was allocated to Personnel expenses and has gone through the accounts for June.

As you know only staff members (not partners/clients etc) attended the Ball.

MEMORANDUM

To: Accountant
From: Assistant accountant
Date: 18 July 20X3
Subject: Supplies received and supplies made

I have established that the only supply received which can be attributed to particular supplies made is the computer bureau services, which are entirely attributable to stockbroking.

MEMORANDUM

To: Accountant
From: Credit controller
Date: 17 June 20X3
Subject: Bad debts

One of our clients, A Jones, to whom we have supplied only investment advice, now seems unlikely to pay his outstanding debts to us, so these debts should be written off. A complete list of supplies to this client is as follows.

Due date for payment of debt	Amount including VAT
	£
1.3.X2	724
1.12.X2	830
1.3.X3	680
31.3.X3	520
10.6.X3	327

A Jones paid £1,000 on 15 December 20X2 and £200 on 1 January 20X3 but did not specify which invoices the payments were in respect of.

---

21   VAT 1   **Assessment**

Calculate the VAT on supplies made in the 3 months ended 30 June 20X3.

22   VAT 2   **Assessment**

Calculate the VAT on supplies received for the 3 months ended 30 June 20X3.

| 23 | **VAT 3** | **Assessment** |

Calculate the VAT on the fuel for private use.

| 24 | **VAT 4** | **Assessment** |

How is the understatement of output VAT for the previous 3 month period accounted for?

| 25 | **VAT 5** | **Assessment** |

How is the Staff Summer Ball accounted for (in terms of VAT)?

| 26 | **VAT 6** | **Assessment** |

How much VAT can be claimed immediately under bad debt relief? When can the remaining VAT be claimed?

| 27 | **VAT 7** | **Assessment** |

What is Strode Ltd's recoverable input VAT for the 3 months ended 30 June 20X3?

| 28 | **VAT 8** | **Assessment** |

What is Strode Ltd's output VAT for the 3 months ended 30 June 20X3?

| 29 | **VAT 9** | **Assessment** |

Prepare Strode Ltd's VAT return for the period from 1 April to 30 June 20X3. A blank VAT return is provided below.

Value Added Tax Return

For the period
01 04 X3 to 30 06 X3

For Official Use

Registration number

| 431 9824 79 |

Period

| 06 X3 |

You could be liable to a financial penalty if your completed return and all the VAT payable are not received by the due date.

Due date: 31 07 X3

| For Official Use | |

ATTENTION

If this return and any tax due are not received by the due date you may be liable to a surcharge.

If you make supplies of goods to another EC Member State you are required to complete an EC Sales List (VAT 101).

STRODE LTD
63 FIG STREET
TREETOWN
Tr1 4NF

If you have a general enquiry or need advice please call our National Advice Service on 0845 010 9000

Before you fill in this form please read the notes on the back and the VAT Leaflet *"Filling in your VAT return"*.
Fill in all boxes clearly in ink, and write 'none' where necessary. Don't put a dash or leave any box blank. If there are no pence write "00" in the pence column. Do not enter more than one amount in any box.

			£	p
For official use	VAT due in this period on sales and other outputs	1		
	VAT due in this period on acquisitions from other EC Member States	2		
	Total VAT due (the sum of boxes 1 and 2)	3		
	VAT reclaimed in this period on purchases and other inputs (including acquisitions from the EC)	4		
	Net VAT to be paid to Customs or reclaimed by you (Difference between boxes 3 and 4)	5		
	Total value of sales and all other outputs excluding any VAT. Include your box 8 figure	6		00
	Total value of purchases and all other inputs excluding any VAT. Include your box 9 figure	7		00
	Total value of all supplies of goods and related services, excluding any VAT, to other EC Member States	8		00
	Total value of all acquisitions of goods and related services, excluding any VAT, from other EC Member States	9		00

If you are enclosing a payment please tick this box.	DECLARATION: You, or someone on your behalf, must sign below.
	I, ... declare that the
	(Full name of signatory in BLOCK LETTERS)
	information given above is true and complete.
	Signature .... Date ....
	A false declaration can result in prosecution.

30   VAT 10   Assessment

State how you would justify your claim for bad debt relief if it were to be challenged by HM Customs & Excise.

Lecturers' trial run devolved assessment

Trial run devolved assessment
Lanbergis Hire Ltd

Performance criteria

The following performance criteria are covered in this Lecturers' trial run devolved assessment.

Element 7.1: Prepare and present periodic performance reports

1   Information derived from different units of the organisation is consolidated into the appropriate form.

2   Information derived from different information systems within the organisation is correctly reconciled.

3   When comparing results over time an appropriate method which allows for changing price levels is used.

4   Transactions between separate units of the organisation are accounted for in accordance with the organisation's procedures.

5   Ratios and performance indicators are accurately calculated in accordance with the organisation's procedures.

6   Reports are prepared in the appropriate form and presented to management within required timescales.

Element 7.2: Prepare reports and returns for outside agencies

1   Relevant information is identified, collated and presented in accordance with the conventions and definitions used by outside agencies.

2   Calculations of ratios and performance indicators are accurate.

3   Authorisation for the despatch of completed reports and returns is sought from the appropriate person.

4   Reports and returns are presented in accordance with outside agencies' requirements and deadlines.

Element 7.3: Prepare VAT returns

1   VAT returns are correctly completed using data from the appropriate recording systems and are submitted within the statutory time limits.

2   Relevant inputs and outputs are correctly identified and calculated.

3   Submissions are made in accordance with current legislation.

4   Guidance is sought from the VAT office when required, in a professional manner.

Trial run devolved assessment Lanbergis Hire Ltd

Instructions

This assessment is designed to test your ability to prepare reports and returns.

The situation is provided on page 178.

The tasks to be completed are set out on pages 179 to 184.

The assessment contains a large volume of data which you will require in order to complete the tasks.

Your answers should be set out in the answer booklet, on pages 187 to 193, using the answer sheets provided.

You are allowed **three hours** to complete your work.

A high level of accuracy is required.

Correcting fluid may be used, but it should be used in moderation. Errors should be crossed out neatly and clearly. You should write in black ink, not pencil.

The information you require is provided as far as possible in the sequence in which you will need to deal with it. However, you are advised to look quickly through all of the material before you begin. This will help you to familiarise yourself with the situation and the information available.

You are reminded that you should not use any unauthorised material, such as books or notes during this Lecturers' trial run devolved assessment.

A full answer to this assessment is provided in the lecturers' resource pack for unit 7.

BPP PUBLISHING

LANBERGIS HIRE LTD

THE SITUATION

Your name is Eric Kendall. You are employed as a temporary accountant by Lanbergis Hire Ltd of 71 Marefair, Lanbergis Outcastle XA32 7DD. You have been engaged to provide holiday cover for Barbara Mandeville, the Accountant, who reports to Raju Shah, the Managing Director of Lanbergis Hire Ltd. Barbara is on holiday from 7 to 22 August 2002.

The company rents out cars to business and private customers, on a daily and weekly basis, as well as hiring out cars on long-term leases.

Lanbergis Hire Ltd's customers must pay for all petrol consumed, in addition to the rental or leasing charge.

Lanbergis Hire Ltd, is a wholly owned subsidiary company of Ghent & Cheny Plc.

Lanbergis Hire Ltd shares the 71 Marefair site with another Ghent & Cheny subsidiary, Outcastle Auto Ltd. Outcastle Auto Ltd has several car repair workshops in the district, though its main workshop is at 71 Marefair.

Outcastle Auto Ltd has its own Managing Director, Wendy Clarke, but some administrative functions are carried out by Lanbergis Hire Ltd on Outcastle Auto Ltd's behalf. There is a considerable amount of inter-company trading, with Lanbergis Hire Ltd's cars being repaired by Outcastle Auto and Lanbergis Hire providing courtesy cars for Outcastle Auto Ltd.

Lanbergis Hire Ltd and Outcastle Auto Ltd are registered as a group for VAT purposes. Lanbergis Hire Ltd acts as the representative member of the group. The company's local VAT office is at 2nd Floor, Tower Chambers, 31 Skew Road, Kirkmanor XA3 9TY.

Lanbergis Hire Ltd's VAT registration number is 578 4060 21.

The financial year end for all Ghent & Cheny group companies is 30 June.

Today's date is Monday 16 August 2002.

Tasks

1 Raju Shah is reviewing Lanbergis Hire Ltd's charges for daily and weekly car hire. The company has not changed its prices since September 2001. Raju has asked you, in Barbara's absence, to investigate the changes in UK motoring costs since September 2001. Raju will then compare this data with Lanbergis Hire's own changes in costs since September 2001.

Raja has asked you to produce separate figures for running costs and for car purchase prices.

Set out below is an extract showing Retail Prices Indexes for the years 2001-2002.

	Group and sub-group weights in 2001	2001 Sep	2001 Oct	2001 Nov	2001 Dec	2002 Jan	2002 Feb	2002 Mar	2002 Apr
Motoring expenditure	139	171.5	170.6	169.6	168.0	169.6	169.4	172.4	175.8
Purchase of motor vehicles	58	139.2	137.9	136.6	134.6	137.1	137.0	136.8	137.1
Maintenance of motor vehicles	23	196.8	197.0	197.0	197.4	198.4	198.7	199.6	200.7
Petrol and oil	38	192.7	192.2	190.7	188.0	186.3	185.5	196.1	206.4
Vehicle tax and insurance	20	213.3	211.3	211.3	211.3	217.5	217.5	220.0	224.9

You are required to construct an index of vehicle running costs, excluding depreciation, petrol and oil, by combining the index for the maintenance of motor vehicles with that for vehicle tax and insurance.

Use the weights contained in the above table.

Enter your results in the form on page 187 of the answer booklet.

2 You are required to take the 'Vehicle running costs index' that you created in Task 1 and re-base it, with September 2001 as 100.

Do the same for the 'Purchase of motor vehicles index'.

Enter your indices in the form contained on page 187 of the answer booklet.

BPP PUBLISHING

3   You are required to write a short informal report to Raju explaining what you have done and noting your findings.

Refer to the table that you produced in Task 2, which you will submit as an attachment to your report.

Give two reasons why the motoring expenditure index contained in the data for Task 1 would not provide a reliable comparison with the changes in the costs to Lanbergis Hire of operating its fleet of hire cars.

Briefly explain how a single index could be calculated from the components used to construct the motoring expenditure index which would reflect more accurately Lanbergis Hire's cost structure and so provide a better basis for comparison with its own cost changes.

Use the memo form on page 188 of the answer booklet. Continue on a separate sheet if necessary.

4   Kirkmanor District Council levy charges for the collection and disposal of industrial waste. The charge is based on a formula combining the volume and tonnage of waste collected with the business's value added figure. Whilst Kirkmanor District Council has its own data for the weight and volume of waste collected from each location, it needs data on the value added by the businesses at each location to calculate the correct charge. It obtains this information by issuing a questionnaire every half year.

You are given the following data for the six months ended 30 June 2002. All figures exclude VAT.

	Lanbergis Hire Ltd	Outcastle Auto Ltd
	£	£
Turnover	1,427,602	1,398,717
Sales to Outcastle Auto included in turnover	18,376	
Sales to Lanbergis Hire included in turnover		43,524
Disposals of capital goods included in turnover	89,320	1,513
Purchases of goods and services, including inter-company transactions	1,042,836	972,374
Purchases of capital goods included in 'purchases of goods and services'	382,718	19,421

You are required to complete the questionnaire on page 189 of the answer booklet in respect of the activities carried out at 71 Marefair.

The value added figure for both businesses should be combined.

Exclude any inter-company trading between Lanbergis Hire and Outcastle Auto.

5   You are required to write a memo to Raju Shah seeking his signature and authority to despatch the value added questionnaire to Kirkmanor District Council.

Alert Raju to the due date for the return of the questionnaire.

BPP PUBLISHING

6   One set of measures of operating efficiency employed by Lanbergis Hire are the percentage availability and utilisation of its vehicles. These figures are calculated weekly.

Two figures are produced

- Availability, defined as 'car-days' available for hiring or leasing as a percentage of car-days in Lanbergis Hire Ltd's ownership

- Hire days as a percentage of available car-days.

The week runs from Monday to Sunday. Lanbergis Hire Ltd are open seven days a week.

Lanbergis Hire Ltd had 72 cars on its books at the beginning of last week.

During that week one car was written off in an accident on Tuesday evening. Ownership immediately passed to Lanbergis Hire Ltd's insurance company under the terms of their policy.

Another car broke down early on Wednesday morning. It was still being repaired in Outcastle Auto Ltd's workshop at the end of the week.

Lanbergis Hire Ltd took delivery of six new cars early on Tuesday morning, these were given a pre-hire service by Outcastle Auto Ltd during Tuesday and Wednesday and were handed over to clients on long-term leases on Thursday morning.

Four cars were sold on Friday afternoon. They were taken out of service on Thursday morning for pre-sale cleaning and servicing by Outcastle Auto Ltd.

Sixteen cars were on long-term leases at the beginning of the week .

One car was returned on Wednesday evening when its lease expired. It was one of the four cars which were sold on Friday.

During the week there were the following short-term rentals, in addition to the long-term leasings.

- 33 one-day hirings

- 34 two-day hirings

- 15 three-day hirings

- 8 four-day hirings

- 4 five-day hirings

- 2 six-day hirings

- 17 seven-day hirings

You are required to complete last week's vehicle utilisation report.

Use the form on page 191 of the answer booklet.

7   Ghent & Cheny Plc has an American subsidiary company, San Luis Exchange Inc. Cary Levinson, one of San Luis Exchange Inc.'s overseas sales staff is about to conduct a protracted business tour of Scandinavia and Northern Europe, including the UK, where he also plans to take a holiday.

Lanbergis Hire Ltd has a car belonging to Harller AB, a Swedish member of the Ghent & Cheny Group which is also a car hire business. The car was left in England by a customer of Harller AB on 7 August 2002. It would normally cost approximately £800 to have the car returned to Sweden.

As Cary is visiting Lanbergis Hire Ltd on 18 August it has been agreed that he can return the car to Harller AB. Cary is particularly keen on the arrangement as he dislikes right-hand drive cars. However, in the absence of the Harller AB car, company policy would dictate that Cary would have to hire a car from Lanbergis Hire Ltd.

Cary will take possession of the car on 18 August as he intends to use it during a holiday in Scotland. He will then use the car while visiting clients in Britain, Denmark, Norway and Sweden, before handing it back to Harller AB. Cary estimates that this arrangement will save San Luis Exchange Inc. about £600 and himself about £400 in car rental fees.

The accounting for this car rental/delivery activity appears complex. Raju Shah has suggested two alternative charging options to recover the loss of the car rental which San Luis Exchange and Cary would otherwise have paid.

*   Lanbergis Hire Ltd to charge San Luis Exchange Inc. £1,000, and San Luis Exchange Inc. to charge Harller AB £800

*   Lanbergis Hire Ltd to charge Harller AB £800 and San Luis Exchange Inc. £200.

It would be left to San Luis Exchange Inc., in either case, to recover the value of the private use from Cary if the company wished.

You are required to write to the local VAT office explaining the situation and seeking their advice as to how each option should be treated for VAT.

Use the blank letterhead provided on page 192 of the answer booklet. Use a continuation sheet if necessary.

8   Barbara Mandeville extracted the following figures from Lanbergis Hire Ltd's and Outcastle Auto Ltd's accounting records as she intended to complete the VAT return before she went on holiday.

In the event, the job was not done and it has been left to you to prepare the VAT return for Barbara's signature when she gets back.

All figures relate to the period 1 May 2002 to 31 July 2002.

There were no purchases from, or sales to, EC or overseas suppliers or customers.

A cheque for any VAT due will accompany the completed return.

	Lanbergis Hire Ltd £	Outcastle Auto Ltd £
Turnover, excluding VAT	815,928.42	699,358.57
Sales to Outcastle Auto included in turnover	12,736.00	
Sales to Lanbergis Hire included in turnover		28,452.75
Disposals of cars, including VAT, not included in turnover	38,187.50	
Purchases, including inter-company transactions, excluding VAT	494,814.67	476,781.92
VAT on purchases	74,212.70	71,517.15
Cars purchased, excluding VAT, not included in 'purchases'	189,723.00	
VAT on cars purchased.	33,201.52	

Notes.

All supplies by both companies were subject to VAT at the standard rate.

All cars were purchased for use as hire cars or for leasing to customers.

You are required to complete the VAT return on page 193 of the answer booklet.

Answer booklet for lecturers' trial run devolved assessment

ANSWER BOOKLET FOR LECTUERS' TRIAL RUN DEVOLVED ASSESSMENT
LANBERGIS HIRE LTD

Task 1

Vehicle running costs index, 13 January 1989 = 100

Year	2001	2001	2001	2001	2002	2002	2002	2002
Month	Sep	Oct	Nov	Dec	Jan	Feb	Mar	Apr
Vehicle running costs index								

Task 2

**Purchase of motor vehicles index and Vehicle running costs index
Re-based to September 2001 =100**

Year	2001	2001	2001	2001	2002	2002	2002	2002
Month	Sep	Oct	Nov	Dec	Jan	Feb	Mar	Apr
Purchase of motor vehicles index, Sep 2001 = 100								
Vehicle running costs index, Sep 2001 = 100								

BPP PUBLISHING

Task 3

MEMO

To:

From:

Subject:

Date:

_____

_____

_____

_____

_____

_____

_____

_____

_____

_____

_____

_____

_____

_____

_____

_____

_____

_____

Task 3

Task 4

Kirkmanor District Council
Environmental Services Department
Town Hall, Kirkmanor XA3 9RS

Value Added Questionnaire - Strictly Confidential

The following information is required to enable the charge for the collection of industrial and commercial waste to be calculated. Failure to reply within 60 days of the designated period end will result in an estimated charge which may exceed considerably that which would normally be payable.

Where waste from more than one business is collected from the same location it will be necessary to consolidate the figures for all businesses operating from that location.

This questionnaire must be completed twice per calendar year, in respect of the six-month period ending 30 June and again in respect of the six month period ending 31 December. In the case of commencement or cessation of a business the questionnaire should be completed to or from the half-year date closest to the date of commencement or cessation.

Company or Business Name(s)	
Full postal address of location from which waste is collected.	
Period covered by this questionnaire	
Turnover, excluding VAT	£
Value added	£

For the purposes of this questionnaire
- *Turnover* should exclude the proceeds from the disposal of capital goods, land and buildings, and all transactions between businesses operating from the same location.
- *Capital goods* are defined as fixed assets which are eligible for capital allowances in the calculation of income tax or corporation tax.
- *Value added* is defined as Turnover, excluding VAT, less Purchased Inputs excluding VAT.
- *Purchased inputs* should exclude purchases of capital goods, land and buildings and transactions between businesses operating from the same location.

Signature of authorised person	Date
Name	Position

The information contained in this questionnaire is confidential and will not be used for any other purpose.

Task 5

MEMO

To:

From:

Subject:

Date:

_____

_____

_____

_____

_____

_____

_____

_____

_____

_____

_____

_____

_____

_____

_____

_____

_____

_____

Task 5

Task 6

<table>
<tr><td colspan="2" align="center">LANBERGIS HIRE LTD

VEHICLE UTILISATION REPORT

WEEK ENDING Sunday ....</td></tr>
<tr><td>1. Car-days in company ownership</td><td></td></tr>
<tr><td>2. Car-days unavailable due to servicing & repairs</td><td></td></tr>
<tr><td>3. Car-days available for hire or leasing (1 minus 2)</td><td></td></tr>
<tr><td>4. Availability percentage (3 as % of 1)</td><td></td></tr>
<tr><td>5. Car-days on long-term leases</td><td></td></tr>
<tr><td>6. Car-days on short-term rentals</td><td></td></tr>
<tr><td>7. Car-days hired out or leased (5 plus 6)</td><td></td></tr>
<tr><td>8. Hire-days percentage (7 as % of 3)</td><td></td></tr>
<tr><td>Report completed by:</td><td>Date:</td></tr>
</table>

Notes.
1. The percentages are to be expressed to one decimal place.
2. Do not use fractions of days. Events occurring before midday are treated as occurring at 00.01 hours. Events occurring after midday are treated as occurring at 24.00 hours.

BPP
PUBLISHING

Task 7

Lanbergis Hire Ltd
71 Marefair, Lanbergis Outcastle XA32 7DD
Telephone 01898-883567

_____

_____

_____

_____

_____

_____

_____

_____

_____

_____

_____

_____

_____

_____

_____

_____

_____

_____

_____

Registered office: 71 Marefair, Lanbergis Outcastle XA32 7DD
Registered in England, number 2314563

Task 7

Task 8

Value Added Tax Return
For the period
01 05 02 to 31 07 02

For Official Use

Registration number | Period
578 4060 21 | 07 02

You could be liable to a financial penalty if your completed return and all the VAT payable are not received by the due date.

Due date: 31 08 02

For Official Use

ATTENTION

If this return and any tax due are not received by the due date you may be liable to a surcharge.

If you make supplies of goods to another EC Member State you are required to complete an EC Sales List (VAT 101).

Barbara Mandeville   Q35192
Lanbergis Ltd
71 Marefair
Lanbergis Outcastle
XA32 7DD   219921/10

If you have a general enquiry or need advice please call our National Advice Service on 0845 010 9000

Before you fill in this form please read the notes on the back and the VAT Leaflet *"Filling in your VAT return"*. Fill in all boxes clearly in ink, and write 'none' where necessary. Don't put a dash or leave any box blank. If there are no pence write "00" in the pence column. Do not enter more than one amount in any box.

For official use			£	p
VAT due in this period on sales and other outputs	**1**			
VAT due in this period on acquisitions from other EC Member States	**2**			
Total VAT due (the sum of boxes 1 and 2)	**3**			
VAT reclaimed in this period on purchases and other inputs (including acquisitions from the EC)	**4**			
Net VAT to be paid to Customs or reclaimed by you (Difference between boxes 3 and 4)	**5**			
Total value of sales and all other outputs excluding any VAT. Include your box 8 figure	**6**			00
Total value of purchases and all other inputs excluding any VAT. Include your box 9 figure	**7**			00
Total value of all supplies of goods and related services, excluding any VAT, to other EC Member States	**8**			00
Total value of all acquisitions of goods and related services, excluding any VAT, from other EC Member States	**9**			00

If you are enclosing a payment please tick this box.

DECLARATION: You, or someone on your behalf, must sign below.

I, ... declare that the
(Full name of signatory in BLOCK LETTERS)
information given above is true and complete.

Signature .... Date ....
A false declaration can result in prosecution.

F

IB (October 2000)

See overleaf for information on other
BPP products and how to order

AAT Order

To BPP Publishing Ltd, Aldine Place, London W12 8AW
Tel: 020 8740 2211. Fax: 020 8740 1184
E-mail: Publishing@bpp.com Web:www.bpp.com

Mr/Mrs/Ms (Full name)

Daytime delivery address

Postcode

E-mail

Daytime Tel

	5/02 Texts	5/02 Kits	Special offer	8/02 Passcards	Tapes
FOUNDATION (£14.95 except as indicated)					
Units 1 & 2 Receipts and Payments	☐	☐	Foundation	£6.95 ☐	£10.00 ☐
Unit 3 Ledger Balances and Initial Trial Balance	☐				
Unit 4 Supplying Information for Mgmt Control	☐				
Unit 20 Working with Information Technology (£9.95) (6/02)	☐				
Unit 22/23 Healthy Workplace/Personal Effectiveness (£9.95)	☐				
INTERMEDIATE (£9.95)					
Unit 5 Financial Records and Accounts	☐	☐	All	£5.95 ☐	£10.00 ☐
Unit 6 Cost Information	☐	☐	Inter'te Texts	£5.95 ☐	£10.00 ☐
Unit 7 Reports and Returns	☐	☐	and Kits (£65)	£5.95 ☐	
Unit 21 Using Information Technology	☐	☐	☐	£5.95 ☐	
TECHNICIAN (£9.95)					
Unit 8/9 Core Managing Costs and Allocating Resources	☐	☐	Set of 12	£5.95 ☐	£10.00 ☐
Unit 10 Core Managing Accounting Systems	☐	☐	Technician		
Unit 11 Option Financial Statements (A/c Practice)	☐	☐	Texts/Kits	£5.95 ☐	£10.00 ☐
Unit 12 Option Financial Statements (Central Govnmt)	☐	☐	(Please		
Unit 15 Option Cash Management and Credit Control	☐	☐	specify titles	£5.95 ☐	
Unit 16 Option Evaluating Activities	☐	☐	required)	£5.95 ☐	
Unit 17 Option Implementing Auditing Procedures	☐	☐	(£100)	£5.95 ☐	
Unit 18 Option Business Tax (FA02)(8/02 Text & Kit)	☐	☐	☐	£5.95 ☐	
Unit 19 Option Personal Tax (FA 02)(8/02 Text & Kit)	☐	☐		£5.95 ☐	
TECHNICIAN 2001 (£9.95)					
Unit 18 Option Business Tax FA01 (8/01 Text & Kit)	☐	☐			
Unit 19 Option Personal Tax FA01 (8/01 Text & Kit)	☐	☐			
SUBTOTAL	£	£	£	£	£

TOTAL FOR PRODUCTS £ ☐

POSTAGE & PACKING

Texts/Kits

	First	Each extra
UK	£2.00	£2.00
Europe*	£4.00	£2.00
Rest of world	£20.00	£10.00

Passcards

UK	£2.00	£1.00
Europe*	£2.50	£1.00
Rest of world	£15.00	£8.00

Tapes

UK	£1.00	£1.00
Europe*	£1.00	£1.00
Rest of world	£4.00	£4.00

£ ☐
£ ☐
£ ☐
£ ☐
£ ☐
£ ☐
£ ☐
£ ☐
£ ☐

TOTAL FOR POSTAGE & PACKING £ ☐
(Max £10 Texts/Kits/Passcards)

Grand Total (Cheques to *BPP Publishing*) I enclose

a cheque for (incl. Postage) £ ☐

Or charge to Access/Visa/Switch

Card Number ☐☐☐☐☐☐

Expiry date _____ Start Date _____

Issue Number (Switch Only) _____

Signature _____

We aim to deliver to all UK addresses inside 5 working days; a signature will be required. Orders to all UK addresses should be delivered within 6 working days. All other orders to overseas addresses should be delivered within 8 working days. * Europe includes the Republic of Ireland and the Channel Islands.

REVIEW FORM & FREE PRIZE DRAW

All original review forms from the entire BPP range, completed with genuine comments, will be entered into one of two draws on 31 January 2003 and 31 July 2003. The names on the first four forms picked out on each occasion will be sent a cheque for £50.

Name: _____ **Address**: _____

_____

_____

How have you used this Assessment Kit?
(Tick one box only)

☐ Home study (book only)

☐ On a course: college _____

☐ With 'correspondence' package

☐ Other _____

Why did you decide to purchase this Assessment Kit? *(Tick one box only)*

☐ Have used BPP Texts in the past

☐ Recommendation by friend/colleague

☐ Recommendation by a lecturer at college

☐ Saw advertising

☐ Other _____

During the past six months do you recall seeing/receiving any of the following?
(Tick as many boxes as are relevant)

☐ Our advertisement in *Accounting Technician* magazine

☐ Our advertisement in *Pass*

☐ Our brochure with a letter through the post

Which (if any) aspects of our advertising do you find useful?
(Tick as many boxes as are relevant)

☐ Prices and publication dates of new editions

☐ Information on Interactive Text content

☐ Facility to order books off-the-page

☐ None of the above

Have you used the companion Interactive Text for this subject? ☐ **Yes** ☐ **No**

Your ratings, comments and suggestions would be appreciated on the following areas

	Very useful	Useful	Not useful
Introductory section (How to use this Assessment Kit etc)	☐	☐	☐
Practice activities	☐	☐	☐
Practice devolved assessments	☐	☐	☐
Trial run devolved assessments	☐	☐	☐
AAT Sample Simulation	☐	☐	☐
Lecturers' Resource Pack activities	☐	☐	☐
Content of answers	☐	☐	☐
Layout of pages	☐	☐	☐
Structure of book and ease of use	☐	☐	☐

	Excellent	Good	Adequate	Poor
Overall opinion of this Kit	☐	☐	☐	☐

Do you intend to continue using BPP Assessment Kits/Interactive Texts? ☐ Yes ☐ No

Please note any further comments and suggestions/errors on the reverse of this page.

The BPP author of this edition can be e-mailed at: lynnwatkins@bpp.com

Please return to: Nick Weller, BPP Publishing Ltd, FREEPOST, London, W12 8BR

REVIEW FORM & FREE PRIZE DRAW (continued)

Please note any further comments and suggestions/errors below

FREE PRIZE DRAW RULES

1   Closing date for 31 January 2003 draw is 31 December 2002. Closing date for 31 July 2003 draw is 30 June 2003.

2   Restricted to entries with UK and Eire addresses only. BPP employees, their families and business associates are excluded.

3   No purchase necessary. Entry forms are available upon request from BPP Publishing. No more than one entry per title, per person. Draw restricted to persons aged 16 and over.

4   Winners will be notified by post and receive their cheques not later than 6 weeks after the relevant draw date.

5   The decision of the promoter in all matters is final and binding. No correspondence will be entered into.